Pronunciati

by Paul Tench

Essential Language Teaching Series

General Editors: Monica Vincent and Roger H Flavell

**MACMILLAN
PUBLISHERS**

1981

First published 1981
Reprinted 1984, 1987, 1991

Published by *Macmillan Publishers Ltd*
London and Basingstoke

ISBN 0–333–27178–5

Typeset by Santype International Ltd, Salisbury, Wilts

Printed in Hong Kong

Contents

1 Teaching pronunciation

1.1 Pronunciation and language teaching

Pronunciation is not an optional extra for the language learner, any more than grammar, vocabulary or any other aspect of language is. If a learner's general aim is to talk intelligibly to others in another language, a reasonable pronunciation is important. A teacher has to give due attention to it along with everything else.

Making yourself understood in a new language involves several different linguistic factors simultaneously. When you say something,

1 it has to be formulated according to the grammatical rules of the language,
2 it has to make sense, with the right choice of vocabulary, idiom and syntactic alternatives,
3 it has to be appropriate to the situation, bearing in mind such matters as who you are speaking to and where,
4 it has to accord with the conventional expression of the particular purpose you have in mind, eg apologising, thanking, complaining, etc,
5 it has to fit in satisfactorily with what has gone on before, *and*
6 it has to be pronounced reasonably well.

All these different factors belong together in anything we say; if any one factor is impaired or wrongly used, then an utterance may well become unintelligible or mean something other than we intended. We can list these factors as: *pronunciation* (or print/handwriting, spelling and punctuation, when the written form is used), *grammar*, *lexis* (vocabulary and idiom), *style* ('appropriate to the situation'), *function* ('purpose you have in mind') and *discourse* ('what has gone on before').

The learner's overall aim and the teacher's overall task should embrace all these factors. The teacher ought to train and equip the learner on all of these levels, and to do that effectively, he often has to abstract one of them for particular attention at any time. But his general aim is to achieve in the learner a certain degree of accuracy and fluency in understanding and responding to the language when it is addressed to him, in either speech or print (or handwriting), and to achieve a degree of accuracy and fluency in expressing himself in the language in both speech and writing. This understanding, responding and expressing is effected on all levels of language simultaneously. This suggests two fundamental principles in the general strategy of pronunciation teaching: on the one hand pronunciation teaching has to be *integrated* with other skills (listening with comprehension, reading and writing, and non-linguistic cues, eg gestures, facial expressions), and with the other aspects of language – grammar, lexis, style, function and discourse; on the other hand, pronunciation has to be *isolated* for practice of specific items and problems, like the articulation of *th*, or various vowels and so on. The second principle serves the first; in order to achieve satisfactory accuracy and fluency of pronunciation, integrated with the other skills and the other aspects of language for successful communication, items of pronunciation need to be isolated for practice and then reintroduced into their context for the successful development of communication.

A simple model of what is involved in any given use of language should make this clear. The various aspects or components of language can be identified and arranged against the various skills of language, as in Table 1 on page 4.

The model is not complete but it is useful for indicating on what levels a person operates when he uses language. For instance, when he listens to somebody, he listens to their sounds (the speaker's pronunciation), he recognises their grammar, vocabulary and style, and he makes an assumption as to the purpose the speaker had in mind (eg was the speaker informing him, questioning him, instructing him, greeting him, etc?). When a person says something, he has to produce sounds, organise his utterance grammatically and lexically, and also appropriately to the context and the situation he is in, and he has a particular purpose in saying what he said. In reading and writing, the operations are very similar; the obvious exception is the substitution of a written representation of language for pronunciation. The twenty-four boxes show the total integration of all components with the four skills; each single box represents an area of language to be isolated for specific practice before being reintroduced into integrated communication. The box marked X is the particular burden of this book.

	Language skills			
Components of Language	Listening	Speaking	Reading	Writing
Pronunciation		X	(Spelling and punctuation)	
Grammar				
Lexis				
Style				
Function				
Discourse				

Table 1

1.2 Pronunciation and phonetics

Pronunciation is not based on spelling. Language is primarily an oral phenomenon, and in many respects (but not in every respect), the written form can be considered as a kind of representation of the spoken. Ideally, the spelling system should closely reflect pronunciation, and in many languages, that indeed is the case. But, alas, it is not the case in English. English spelling is only a poor reflection of English pronunciation, although it must be admitted that there are many regularities between sound and written symbol which it is valuable for the teacher to know.

The nature of the problem is twofold: firstly, each sound of English is represented by more than one written letter or by sequences of letters; and secondly, any letter of English represents more than one sound, or it may not represent any sound at all. The most familiar example of the lack of consistency between spelling and pronunciation is the letter sequence *ough*. Test for yourself the variations that this letter sequence represents in spelling:

though   (rhymes with *slow*)   *cough* (rhymes with *off*)
through (rhymes with *true*)   *tough* (rhymes with *stuff*)
thought (rhymes with *taut*)   *bough* (rhymes with *now*)
thorough (rhymes partially with   *hough* (rhymes with *lock*)
        colour)

Other examples come quickly to mind. The pronunciation of the *sh* sound is spelt variously as in these examples: *ship, passion, ration, Asian, conscious, Confucian, issue, machine, luxury* ($x = k + sh$), *fuschia*. That of *ee* is even more variously spelt: *me, meet, meat, mete, people, grief, grieve, conceit, conceive, key, quay, machine, pizza, amoeba, mediaeval*, and for many people, also the final sound in *city*.

Now consider the letter *i*; how many different pronunciations are there that this letter can represent? *Ink, item, grief, weigh, pier*, *air, first, plaits, fruit, choir, reservoir, ration, soldier* – 13 at least! The lack of consistency between spelling and pronunciation immediately becomes apparent in these four examples; other examples would only confirm it further.

All this serves to warn us that the spelling of a word is not the basis of the pronunciation of the word. Consequently, the teaching of pronunciation should not be based on the written form of language; the written form may act as a kind of support or reinforcement, but *the primary stimulus in pronunciation practice must be the spoken form itself*.

Pronunciation is more than a matter of consonants, vowels and diphthongs. Listen to the sound of people speaking, and listen out for the rise and fall of the pitch of the voice, to the pausing and grouping together of words and phrases, and to the highlighting of some syllables and the virtual suppression of others, and you will *hear* that there is more to pronunciation. Words are indeed represented in speech by consonants, vowels and diphthongs, but by accented and unaccented syllables too. To take a well-known example, *'import* ('precedes the accented syllable) is a noun, but *(to) im'port* is a verb. But beyond that, sentences or, better, utterances display a kind of rhythm and are accompanied by pitch variations, or intonation. A learner is likely to experience difficulties with each of these elements of pronunciation, and help is offered to the teacher on all these aspects in the following chapters. One aspect is not dealt with and that is the expression of paralinguistic features of mood, such as a grumpy voice or speaking sharply and so on; this is too complex a matter and too involved for a short book like this.

Pronunciation, then, is itself a complex of sounds (consonants, vowels and diphthongs), syllables (word accent and rhythm) and intonation, and each element needs attention. The study of the elements of pronunciation is called 'phonetics', and there exist many good handbooks on phonetics in general and on the phonetics of English in particular (see Further reading section, page 118; see also the Glossary of phonetic terms, page 120).

At this point, I wish only to introduce the basic phonetic symbols for discussing English pronunciation teaching. (The scheme and techniques described in this book are however applicable directly to teaching the pronunciation of any language.) Writing down the pronunciation of an utterance with these symbols is known as 'transcription'. This transcription is important in the representation of pronunciation because of the inconsistency in the relationship between pronunciation and spelling. A symbol in the transcription system refers to one sound and that sound only; furthermore that particular sound is represented by that one symbol and by no other; there is a simple one-to-one correspondence between symbol and sound. For instance, /t/ only represents the sound that is spelt *t* in the word *tin*, and never the sound that is spelt *t* in *nation*.

CONSONANTS

Here is a complete list of the consonant symbols for English:

/p/ as in *p*in	/b/ as in *b*in
/t/ as in *t*in	/d/ as in *d*in
/k/ as in *c*oal	/g/ as in *g*oal
/m/ as in *m*eal	/n/ as in *n*ot
/f/ as in *f*ine	/v/ as in *v*ine
/θ/ as in *th*in	/ð/ as in *th*is
/s/ as in *s*eal	/z/ as in *z*eal
/ʃ/ as in *sh*ip	/ʒ/ as in mea*s*ure
/tʃ/ as in *ch*eer	/dʒ/ as in *j*eer
/h/ as in *h*ill	/ŋ/ as in ki*ng*
/l/ as in *l*et	/r/ as in *r*ed
/w/ as in *w*et	/j/ as in *y*et

Note especially that the sound spelt *c* in *coal* is represented by /k/ and /g/ is not used for the sound *g* in *gin*. You need to be careful with /s/ as well; there is, for instance, only one /s/ sound in the word *scissors*, despite its spelling (the -*ss*- and the final -*s* are /z/). Another common problem is associating the /j/ symbol with the sound spelt *j*; /j/ only refers to the *y* sound of words like *yes*, *youth*, and *beyond*, and of words like *unit*, *European* and *news* (/njuz/).

There are a number of extra symbols from outside the range of letters of the English alphabet; the alphabet simply cannot cope adequately with all the 24 consonants and 20 vowels and diphthongs of English. An awkward problem is the representation of the two *th*'s of English; the *th* of *thin* is voiceless and is represented by /θ/, whereas the *th* of *this* is voiced and is represented by a separate symbol, / ð/. Say the two words over and over again until you are convinced of the difference between them. How would you transcribe the *th* of these words: *the*, *these*, *thing*, *them*, *thought*, *weather*, *ether*, *warmth*, *breath*, *breathe*?

The other extra symbols are fairly straightforward: /ʃ/ represents the *sh* sound of *ship*, *passion*, etc (see above); and /ʒ/ the *s* in *treasure* and *vision*, as well as the *ge* in *beige*, *prestige*. The double symbols, /tʃ/ and /dʒ/, indicate the stop and friction sequence in affricates; /tʃ/ represents the *ch* sound of *cheer*, and of *picture*, and /dʒ/ the *j* sound of *jeer*, and of *soldier*. The remaining extra symbol is /ŋ/ which combines the tail of a hand-printed *g* and the *n*, and it represents a nasal at the velar point of articulation: *ng* of *king*, *long*, etc and, incidentally, also the *n* of *think*, *bank*, which also happens to be velar.

VOWELS AND DIPHTHONGS

It is much more difficult to identify the vowels and diphthongs of English because they vary a great deal from accent to accent, and because the relationship between them and spelling is extremely inconsistent, more so than in the case of the consonants. A set of transcription symbols is vital for the description of vowels and diphthongs because the principle of one-to-one correspondence between symbol and sound offers the only sensible way of representing them.

Here is a complete list of the vowel and diphthong symbols for standard English:

/i/ as in bead	/ɪ/ as in bid
/e/ as in bed	/æ/ as in bad
/ɑ/ as in bard	/ʌ/ as in bud
/ɔ/ as in bored	/ɒ/ as in pod
/ʊ/ as in good	/u/ as in booed
/ɜ/ as in bird	/ə/ as in cupboard
/ɑɪ/ as in bide	/ɑʊ/ as in cowed
/eɪ/ as in paid	/əʊ/ as in bode
/ɔɪ/ as in boy	/ɪə/ as in beard
/eə/ as in bared	/ʊə/ as in poured

A word of caution must be added immediately. The pronunciation of these words corresponds to a particular accent of English, and your own pronunciation may be different in some cases. It may be different because you use a different vowel from the one given above, eg many people pronounce *bored* and *poured* in such a way that they rhyme – but they do not rhyme in every accent. Your pronunciation may also be different because you use a diphthong instead of a vowel, or a vowel instead of a diphthong. For example, many people in Wales, Scotland and the north of England would not have a diphthong in words like *paid* and *bode*; that is, instead of the slight gliding movement of the tongue, there would be a relatively stable or pure vowel, which would also be quite long. Others would have a clearly diphthongal articulation for the /i/ vowel; people from the urban Midlands have such a pronunciation. Other likely areas of differences will be mentioned later.

There is one particular feature of the vowels of English that we need to mention. Some vowels are discernibly longer than others. Take the words *bead* and *bid*; say them a few times and listen for the relative length of the two vowels. You should be able to hear that the /i/ of *bead* is longer than the /ɪ/ of *bid*. This goes for other pairs of vowels: comparing the vowel sounds of *food* and *good*, the /u/ of *food* can be heard to be longer than the /ʊ/ of *good*; the /ɑ/ of *hard* is longer than the /æ/ of *had*; the /ɔ/ of *cord* is longer than the /ɒ/ of *cod*; and /ɜ/ is longer than /ə/. The first vowel in each of these pairings is often referred to as a *long vowel*, and the others, along with /e/ and /ʌ/, as *short vowels*. This lengthening of vowels is conventionally indicated by a colon (:), and thus the five long vowels have been transcribed by many linguists and teachers as /iː, ɑː, ɔː, uː, ɜː/. The only problem that this gives to the unwary is that in older transcriptions, the short vowels were usually indicated by the symbol of the nearest long vowel, but without the colon. Now, this can be really confusing, because the transcription /bid/ represents *bead* in most recent publications, but *bid* in older publications. It is therefore vital that you make sure exactly what the symbols stand for whenever you use a phonetics dictionary or reference book or teaching materials that include phonetic transcriptions.

NB The word 'sound' is not really precise because, in fact, the *sound* /t/ includes quite a number of different sounds. The *t* of *sting* is different from the *t* of *tin* – the first is unaspirated, the second aspirated (look up 'aspiration' in the Glossary of phonetic terms, if you are unsure of the meaning of these terms). If you say the two words carefully and slowly and listen for the difference, it will become quite clear. You might then be able to detect yet another type of *t* in *train*, where the tongue bends back because of the following *r* (see also page 67). Such variations are typical of all the sounds given in the above lists, and many linguists prefer to use the term 'phoneme' to refer to the cluster of sound variations that make up a single unit in the pronunciation system. That single unit is the phoneme; so we can refer to /t/ as a phoneme of English and note that it involves a certain range of minute variations that are called 'allophones' (or 'allophonic' variations). The symbols in the above lists represent the phonemes of English, and each phoneme involves a number of minute variations (which receive attention in Chapters 3 and 4). The phoneme symbols are conventionally enclosed between slanting brackets, //.

1.3 Varieties of pronunciation

No language is uniform; every language varies in different ways as a result of different factors. This is true of all levels of language and not just pronunciation. The most obvious factor in language variation is geography; language varies from area to area and this accounts for what we call 'regional dialects'. The pronunciation aspect of dialect is referred to as accent, and we have to decide which accent or accents are important and which one will form the basis of our teaching.

A language also varies gradually in time – *generation* varieties. Our grandparents do not speak in quite the way we do; there are differences in pronunciation. A language also varies socially; there are *social* varieties. People in the so-called professions do not talk in the same way as members of the working class. This is not to decry the speech of the working class, but simply an observation that such varieties exist. Pronunciation is the most obvious clue to social background. A doctor and a docker from the same area will be *expected* to speak differently, and it would certainly sound very strange to hear a trade-union official speaking like an Anglican bishop! Language varies between men and women – varieties based on *sex*. These may not be so obvious, but men would generally avoid using words that they associate with women's speech, eg calling a person 'sweet'. This is also true in pronunciation – men do not like to sound like women! There are *idiosyncratic* varieties too as a result of a slight defect or a particular upbringing. *Temperamental* varieties also exist; the cool, calm and collected type of person *sounds* different from the tense, nervous type. And finally, and more importantly, there are *stylistic* varieties – the way we respond to particular sets of circumstances.

The most common classification of styles is into formal, colloquial and rapid colloquial, and the reasons for changing from one style to another are mainly matters of who a person is talking to and in what setting. A formal style would be typical of the situation where someone is addressing a group of people at a meeting, or when someone is addressing somebody unfamiliar to him and recognises that in some way that person has a higher status than himself. Formal speech is relatively slow and careful. Colloquial speech is typical of people addressing others they regard as colleagues or equals in informal circumstances; it is usually quicker and less careful than formal speech. Rapid colloquial speech is, of course, even quicker and even less careful and is used between close friends in relaxed or intimate circumstances. Of all the types of language varieties, the most important for the language teacher, as far as pronunciation is concerned, are accent and these stylistic variations. The aim of a language learner in this latter respect would be to choose the appropriate style for any occasion.

Whatever kind of pronunciation we eventually decide to teach, it is quite obvious that we will not be able to describe in this chapter all the varieties that we have hinted at. The usual procedure in this case is to describe one variety and compare the other varieties with it. The variety we will select for description is the variety that is based on the pronunciation of educated, professional people of the south-eastern part of Britain, of the middle generation, who are temperamentally stable and free of idiosyncratic features, speaking colloquially! Now, why choose them? Because it is their speech that has been subjected to the most detailed investigation and which appears in all manuals and dictionaries of pronunciation published in Britain. It is also the kind of pronunciation that has consistently appeared in text-books for students of English as a foreign or second language. So whether a prospective English-language speaker speaks that variety or not, he needs at least to be acquainted with a description of it. Linguists have referred to it variously as Received Pronunciation, Educated Southern English and Southern British Standard. It is also often popularly called the Oxford accent, or the BBC accent. In fact, the best way to refer to it is to refer to the accent of news broadcasters on the radio and television of the BBC and ITV.

"He's on a temporary attachment."

The number of consonants is usually pretty much the same whatever the accent, and so there is not usually any difficulty in recognising them. But the number and actual pronunciation of the vowels can vary quite a lot from accent to accent. Some differences were mentioned on page 9. In fact, very many people do not have a diphthong in their pronunciation that corresponds to the Received Pronunciation /ʊə/. It occurs in words like *poor*, *moor*, *cure*, *endure*. If you pronounce *poor* and *moor* identically to *pour* and *more*, and if your pronunciation of *cure* and *endure* rhyme with *yore*, then it is quite likely that you do not possess the

/ʊə/ diphthong at all in your speech. Moreover, many people do not pronounce /eə/ as a diphthong, but rather as a kind of prolonged /e/. Test your pronunciation of words like *air*, *care*, *there*; is there any gliding movement of your tongue? If there is, then it is the diphthong; if not, it is the prolonged type of /e/.

Another type of accent variation can be illustrated from the way you pronounce words like *class*, *laugh* and *aunt*. Does your pronunciation of *class* make it rhyme with *farce* (as it does in Received Pronunciation) or with *gas* (as it does for most English speakers)? Do you pronounce *laugh* to rhyme with *scarf* (Received Pronunciation)? For some, *aunt* is pronounced like *aren't* (Received Pronunciation), but for most English speakers, it is pronounced like *ant*. Similar examples involve words like *cut* and *put*, and *luck*, *look* and *Luke*.

/ʌ/ and /ə/ often cause problems; if you make a distinction between *unending* and *an ending*, it will most probably be because you have used /ʌ/ at the beginning of the first, and /ə/ for the (unaccented) *an*. Compare also *up-end*, which begins with /ʌ/ in Received Pronunciation, and *append*, which begins with /ə/; *humdrum* ends with /ʌ/, whereas *conundrum* ends with /ə/. However, in many dialects, there is in fact no difference. (Say these examples and the key words of the vowel list over and over again and feel the difference in tongue position for each vowel. Note that the vowels /u, ʊ, ɔ, ɒ/, have a certain degree of lip rounding.)

Another type of pronunciation difference is whether *r* is pronounced at the end of words. It just so happens that English people on the whole stopped pronouncing the final *-r* of words like *poor*, *fair*, *fear*, *far*, *fir*, *four* and *liver* during the eighteenth century; but, nevertheless, people in the south-west of England, and in Scotland and America have continued to do so. This means that whereas for most people in England today, such *r*'s are silent when the words they occur in are said in isolation, they may not be for you, if you come from one of the places just mentioned.

This affects your pronunciation of the vowels, and you may well have a much simpler vowel system than Received Pronunciation. Still, you need to know Received Pronunciation because, although you may pronounce *nurse, worse, verse, first,* and *hearse* with different vowels, your textbook will treat them as all having the same vowel, /ɜ/, the vowel in Received Pronunciation. (This is not to say that your pronunciation, therefore, *has* to conform; only that you need to be aware of such differences to avoid unnecessary confusion in your teaching.) Non-native speaker teachers of English similarly must be aware of differences between their pronunciation and Received Pronunciation.

1.4 Model of pronunciation

The variety of pronunciation that has gained a particular social status is the form that was referred to in the previous section as Received Pronunciation (or RP for short). Should this be the form, the 'model' accent, that you should teach? We will consider arguments for and against.

RP is the British accent that has been analysed in greatest detail. British descriptions of pronunciation and British pronouncing dictionaries invariably use that form, and the pronunciation given in any other British dictionary is RP. It is associated with educated people and has been associated in the past and to a certain extent still today with influential people – in politics, religion, business and education. All British textbooks designed for the teaching of English as a second or foreign language also invariably use RP. Many employers expect an English-language teacher to speak RP, and the form that learners will hear on the news and many other programmes on radio and television will be RP. Tape-recordings that accompany textbooks usually have RP speakers exclusively. The weight of argument in favour of RP appears to be overwhelming, but there are problems that need considering.

One problem probably became obvious as you read the preceding paragraph: the word 'British'. There are more Americans than Britons who speak English! And there are as many Americans teaching English as there are Britons. In some parts of the world, traditional American influence will make an American form of pronunciation more useful – Latin America and parts of the Far East, for instance, and in many oil-rich countries of the Middle East where American personnel in the oil industry strongly outnumber the British. The American presence in Europe, in business and the armed forces, is influential enough to be a rival to RP there. Then, of course, American textbooks and dictionaries all present what is commonly called General American (GA for short), and the tape-recordings that accompany them have American voices. American radio and films have a great appeal and are widely available. There are other recognisably national and international forms – eg Australian, Indian, West African and Caribbean – and in these places, these forms of pronunciation will have to be reckoned with.

There is another obvious problem. Most English people do not speak RP (although it may be claimed that RP is the largest minority). This may well mean that you yourself do not speak RP. There may well be differences in your pronunciation of certain vowels and diphthongs, possibly also certain consonants; and there may be occasional differences in word accents, especially in those cases where word accents are in the process of changing. If you pronounce 'controversy with the accent on the first syllable, that is in line with RP; if you don't, but say con'troversy, you are probably not an RP speaker.

For many teachers, the differences between their pronunciation and RP are very small and can be safely ignored. Teachers with many differences will find it difficult to switch over completely to RP; it would not be a good plan for them to use their *own* accent for most of their teaching, and then to conduct only pronunciation exercises in RP. It would be better to keep pronunciation consistent throughout every aspect of teaching, and integrate pronunciation activities as far as possible into the rest of the teaching scheme, as is advocated in the next chapter.

Teach an accent that is acceptable as an educated accent and keep it consistently in all your teaching; point out any major differences between RP and American pronunciation in an incidental way. You will need to know RP because of its prevalence in course books; some knowledge of General American would also be useful. This advice is offered to overseas teachers too: if you have been taught to use RP (or GA), use it in your own teaching, otherwise use an acceptable educated accent that is appropriate to where you are teaching.

1.5 Intelligibility

The final question being considered in this opening chapter is: what degree of accuracy, fluency and appropriateness ought to be expected? An obvious answer would seem to be: as good as the native speaker of the language. But that might be, literally, a counsel of perfection, and for many learners it may simply be unattainable or impracticable. It may not even be necessary or desirable even if it was practically possible, because most language learners have modest ambitions and are not perfectionists. Language teachers and professional interpreters ought to aim for the closest approximation to native English speech because of the very nature of their occupations. But an alternative has been proposed by Professor David Abercrombie for the majority of language learners. Instead of perfection, he advocates intelligibility: 'most ... language learners need no more than a comfortably intelligible pronunciation (and by "comfortably" intelligible, I mean a pronunciation which can be understood with little or no conscious effort on the part of the listener). I believe that pronunciation teaching should have, not a goal which must of necessity be normally an unrealized ideal, but a *limited* purpose which will be completely fulfilled: the attainment of intelligibility'. (Abercrombie 1963: 37; italics in original.)

Intelligibility rests on abilities at all levels of language. Intelligibility would be impaired, for instance, if the wrong word was chosen or if some feature of grammar was unrecognisable. It would obviously also be impaired if a word was mispronounced or if a sentence was uttered with odd rhythm and intonation patterns. It is this latter type of threat to intelligibility that we are concerned with here.

Although a word may be mispronounced, there may be enough clues in the linguistic context and in the situation to compensate. If a learner is heard to say, 'I'm going to take the dock for a walk', it is, on the surface, nonsense; but we process the sentence in order to make sense of it and interpret *dock* as *dog*. We interpret in this way because we know, for instance, that we can only take animate beings for a walk and because we are aware of the habit of many people who do take dogs for walks. In other words we interpret the nonsense by reference to the context; if there actually was a dog in the situation, then that would confirm our interpretation. Similarly, if someone says 'I sink so' without there being any reference to sinking in the conversation up to that point or in the situation, then we would not hesitate to interpret it as meaning 'I think so'. However, of course, there may not be enough such clues or any such clues at all to prevent ambiguity or misunderstanding. If, for instance, a learner has not learnt to make the vowel distinction in words like *colour* and *collar*, then he would be misunderstood if he talked about the 'collar of the shirt' when he really meant 'colour'. And, then, if he produces a vowel sound that is half-way between the two vowels of those words, that will lead to ambiguity. In other words, a learner can get away with many pronunciation faults because of the compensation of linguistic and situational clues, but he will not *always* be able to do so.

Two other factors are relevant here. First of all, the *listener's threshold of intelligibility*. The learner's teacher may well have a low threshold of intelligibility; that is, because the teacher knows the kind of mistakes the learner makes and perhaps too because of his experience of teaching many other people, he (the teacher) can often make out what the learner is trying to say. In other words, the learner does not have to reach a very high level for him to cross the teacher's low threshold of intelligibility. On the other hand, somebody else may have had very much less experience of dealing with foreign learners and have, consequently, a high threshold of intelligibility. This means that the learner does have to reach a high standard in order to cross it.

Secondly, the *listener's tolerance*. The tolerance factor may turn out to be a key factor in determining the level or degree which a learner has to aim for in pronunciation. For instance, a learner who is an au pair in an English-speaking family may be fortunate in having listeners with a great deal of tolerance; that is, it may not matter too much if she makes a lot of mistakes or speaks inappropriately at times or hesitates a great deal or has to repeat herself while her listeners search in their minds for what she must have meant. Such listeners would have to show a great deal of tolerance! On the other hand, a conference interpreter is not expected to make mistakes, speak inappropriately, hesitate, have to repeat himself or have to look things up; in other words, he is operating with very little tolerance from his listeners.

The degree of intelligibility that any learner should aim for depends to a large extent on who his expected audience is and on *their* threshold of intelligibility and tolerance. Where the expected audience is vague, general or unknown, the learner must aim at speaking to people with a high threshold of intelligibility and with little tolerance. The best test is actually to speak to such a person; if that person has to strain himself and work hard at trying to understand the learner, then the learner has failed; if, on the other hand, he can understand the learner with little or no conscious effort, then he has passed. He would then have attained the comfortably intelligible pronunciation that Professor Abercrombie recommended.

One final consideration is the matter of *channel*. We have discussed the aims and objectives of the learner so far in terms of conversation or face-to-face contact. Channel is the means by which an utterance is transmitted, and besides face-to-face contact, it includes the telephone, tape-recordings, radio contact and public-address systems. The last two channels may not be relevant for all learners, but would be at least for prospective (or actual) policemen, navigators, dockers, air-traffic controllers and airport announcers. All electronically operated channels normally place extra burdens on the learner's degree of intelligibility.

2   Basic strategy

The basic strategy in pronunciation teaching is imitation, whether we are dealing with beginners or more advanced learners. The learner needs to be able to imitate the teacher's pronunciation of whole utterances in context, imitating not only the features of consonants, vowels and diphthongs, but rhythm and intonation too. He also needs specific practice for certain pronunciation items which he finds awkward and difficult, and this kind of practice receives attention in the following chapters. In this chapter, we will be concentrating on how to work out the basic strategy. I want to take two different teaching situations to illustrate how we might do this, one with beginners and one with more advanced students, and also consider the question of pronunciation in oral drills designed for grammar practice.

I prefer the word 'imitation' to 'repetition', because a learner may reproduce words and utterances without reproducing their sounds; 'imitation' draws attention particularly to the reproduction of sounds. In this sense, it is synonymous with 'mimic', the word which Americans seem to prefer.

2.1 Beginning students

The language-teaching situation I have in mind with beginners is a class of 30 eleven-year-olds in a country where English has no official status and where the children share a common mother tongue. They are beginning a school course of at least four years' duration, and their objective in general terms is to be able to command enough English in all skills to benefit from contacts with native English speakers and from visits to an English-speaking country; the kind of language they will learn is everyday, non-technical, colloquial language. The physical setting of the teaching situation is a classroom in a school and the teacher is equipped with a set of textbooks, blackboard and chalk. Variations of this situation are discussed at the end of this section.

We will take an actual textbook to demonstrate what a teacher might do to encourage good pronunciation from the very first lesson: *Access to English: Starting Out* (Coles & Lord 1974). Chapter 1 contains reading material with coloured and black-and-white illustrations, a dialogue and drills. The reading material focuses on certain grammatical points and sentence structures: *wh*-question with *this* ('what's this?'), a response *It's (it is) a,* a statement with *this* ('This is a town'), the prepositions *of* and *in*, 'yes/no' questions ('Are we in a library?') with affirmative, short responses ('Yes, we are') and follow-up statements ('We're (we are) in a library in Middleford'), vocatives ('Mr Steele, . . .') and the numerals 1–20. The vocabulary of the reading material includes *map*, *town*, *plan*, town buildings, office furnishings, *man*, *woman*, *boy*, *girl*, the Christian names *Arthur* and *Mary*, and the title and the surname *Mr Steele*. The dialogue is a straightforward formal set of greetings. The drills, which are to be conducted orally, include the alphabet and (spoken) spelling, the sequence, 'Ah, you're here. Yes, I'm here' with all the personal pronouns, declarative clauses of the type, 'This is a map', and short answers ('Yes, he is') to 'yes/no' questions ('Is Arthur in Middleford?'). The style of the language is either formal (eg 'What is this?') or colloquial ('What's this?'), which, in these cases, probably also reflects differences between written and spoken forms; the situations include formal ones (assistants with superiors) and informal ones (with equals). The language functions covered are identifying, seeking information and greetings. The teacher's objectives are, in the authors' words, that he 'should satisfy himself that the student can:

1 understand what he hears;
2 produce the new language items effectively in speech;
3 understand what he reads;
4 write intelligibly and accurately'. (Teacher's Edition)

Although we, in this book, are primarily interested in 2 above, we must bear in mind that the teacher is interested *equally* in 1, 2, 3 and 4.

The reading material is clearly meant to be used orally as well, since the form *what is* is supplemented by *what's*, and *it is* is supplemented by *it's*, etc. But the teacher may well want to use the dialogue as the first concentrated pronunciation practice, because that is what is intended to be said, not read. The dialogue runs like this:

Arthur	Good morning, Mr Steele.
Mr Steele	Ah, you're here, Arthur.
Arthur	Yes, I am . . . . Good morning, Mary.
Mary	Good morning, Arthur. How are you?
Arthur	Very well, thank you. And you?
Mary	Fine, thanks.

The teacher is given no directions in the Teacher's Edition about pronunciation teaching although he is encouraged to enable his learners to 'produce the new language items effectively in speech'. The objective of the teacher must be that his learners should reproduce the given dialogue with good pronunciation and should greet him and others effectively, such that the addressee can recognise without difficulty the various parts of the dialogue and respond accordingly. The true test would be whether the learner could greet a native speaker of English successfully.

How should the teacher begin and what should he do? Should the learners have their books open at the appropriate page? If the learners can read (in their mother tongue, that is) and their mother-tongue script is roman (like the English script) then there might be some point in having their books open, with the written text of what they are going to learn to say, in front of them. Learners seem to benefit from knowing where one word ends and the next one begins. The learners have to establish the association between sound and (graphic) symbol at some time or other; it has been shown beyond doubt that where the graphic form has been excluded, learners tend to invent some kind of mental spelling to help them remember individual sounds and the pronunciation of words; this mental spelling has then to be 'unlearned' when standard spelling is introduced and this causes unnecessary extra interference for the learner to cope with.

Reference to the written form during pronunciation practice might be regarded as dangerous, as it might turn pronunciation practice into reading practice, and the lack of consistency between pronunciation and spelling might constitute a hindrance. The first danger can be avoided by making sure that when an individual learner responds in imitation practice, he does not read the text but responds directly to the teacher's spoken stimulus. While he is responding in this way, others may glance down at the printed version; and when he has completed his response, he too is free to glance down, while another is called upon to speak. In this way, the printed version is not a primary stimulus in the imitation procedure, but a secondary stimulus; *it is the teacher's spoken stimulus that is the primary stimulus to the learner*.

The problem of the lack of consistency between spelling and pronunciation can be eased by careful selection and gradation of words; words introduced in the early chapters should reflect as much as possible a stable consistency, and difficulties delayed until later – a well-known pedagogical principle. The problem can be eased but not altogether eliminated – the very first part of language the learner sees in Chapter 1 of *Starting Out* contains the words *what* and *map*, with different values for the letter *a*, and the words *is* and *this* with different values for the letter *s* (this latter difference is, of course, eliminated in the weak form of *is* in *what's*).

Furthermore, the opportunity of an occasional glance at the printed form helps beginners to overcome another problem. If the utterances of the imitation procedure contain more than five or six words or contain a number of polysyllabic words, beginners are likely to stumble before the end of the utterance, or invert the word order, or get a psychological 'block' over a particular word. Also, if, as psychologists suggest, an accurate acoustic image of a word or utterance cannot be retained for longer than 5-10 seconds, then any device that facilitates a response within that time should be encouraged; the printed version does seem to offer such a facility in the case of sentences longer than five or six words, and of sentences with a number of polysyllabic words. Incidentally, if the printed version helps to reduce stumbling, inversion and blocks, it consequently helps to save time and reduce unwanted distractions. The advantages of having the printed version available as a secondary stimulus outweigh the dangers.

If the eleven-year-olds are not literate, reference to the printed version is largely meaningless and should be avoided, at least in the initial stages. And if they are used to a different script, it would also be worth delaying the introduction of the roman script; that would be a separate task. But when the roman script had been introduced, there would then be no reason not to refer to the printed version during pronunciation practice.

Should the learners understand the meaning of what they are practising for pronunciation? In by far the majority of cases, the answer is the obvious one: yes. If the learners are going to proceed from the given dialogue to their own impromptu version, understanding is one of the decisive factors. (Others are the mastery of grammatical features and pronunciation.) In any case, if the learners do not understand the meaning of the utterances they are practising, their attention is divided; they would be trying to perform at least two distinct mental operations. They would be simultaneously trying to concentrate on the phonetic form of the utterance and trying also to accommodate the unfamiliar utterance into their established experience of the world – in other words, they would also be trying to make sense of it to work out the meaning. If the meaning is made clear, it relieves the learner of one of his mental burdens and allows him to concentrate on what the teacher really intends – pronunciation. The meaning can be conveyed by visual aids, such as the illustrations in the textbook, or actions, or by context, or by giving briefly the equivalent in the mother tongue. As it happens in this particular dialogue, understanding the meaning presents no great problems; but a teacher might give brief mother-tongue equivalents to make sure: context may help, but visual aids that indicated unambiguously 'Good morning, Mr Steele' or indicated the fine distinction between 'Very well, thank you' and 'Fine, thanks' would be hard to devise. The illustration that accompanies the dialogue in the book merely provides the setting, rather than the meaning, of the dialogue.

To return to the earlier question: How should the teacher begin and what should he do? He should say the first utterance a few times, and, if he thinks it necessary, he might give the mother-tongue equivalent and possibly explain who *Mr Steele* is. He should say the utterance a few times before expecting any student to respond. He should say the utterance at normal speed because native speakers do not usually greet with slow over-careful articulation; if the teacher knows his phonetics, he will realise that the *d* of *Good* will assimilate to the *m* of *morning* and yield /b/ and it will be realised as [gʊbm ...] rather than [gʊdᵊm ...]. *Good* is mostly unaccented in greetings; the intonation falls on

DIALOGUE

ARTHUR: Good morning, Mr Steele.
MR STEELE: Ah, you're here, Arthur.
ARTHUR: Yes, I am . . . . Good morning, Mary.
MARY: Good morning, Arthur. How are you?
ARTHUR: Very well, thank you. And you?
MARY: Fine, thanks.

Figure 1 Coles & Lord 1974:7

morn-, and, optionally, rises slightly on *Steele*. After saying the utterance a few preliminary times, the teacher should point to one of his learners and get him to imitate without glancing down at the text. The teacher might also consider instructing his learners (in their mother tongue) what they should do; the learner who responds must do so without glancing down at the text and must do so promptly; the rest of the class may glance at the text but should also mouth the response silently to themselves – this mouthing might in fact constitute a kind of semi-active response, and thus make their waiting for their turn more productive. Mouthing is only necessary for beginners and can be abandoned as soon as the learners have mastered all the difficult sounds.

The teacher then points to one learner, who responds, and immediately upon the latter's response gives the utterance again pointing to another. The teacher should attempt to establish a rapid stimulus-response procedure, in order to gain rhythm in the exercise. When the exercise is going with a swing, teacher and learners alike feel that the exercise is going well and effectively, which boosts the learner's confidence, makes the lesson more entertaining and pleasant and thus aids motivation. The teacher should point to individual learners rather than call them by name, so that nothing intervenes in the precious seconds between the teacher's stimulus and the learner's response. If it is felt that pointing alone is unfriendly and negative, it should be borne in mind that it is effective in an intensive procedure, and that there are plenty of opportunities in more relaxed procedures to use names with good effect. Pointing is likely to be inaccurate, however, if the teacher stays at the front of the classroom; he should move freely down the aisles and around the room to be closer to the one he is pointing to, so that the pointing is clear and he can hear the responses better. (See Figure 2.)

Figure 2

The teacher should select learners at random, so that they do not know who is going to be called upon next. This random selection helps to keep learners alert and attentive. There is usually no problem for them to be glancing down at the text and keeping an eye on the teacher's finger in case he points to them. Random selection also helps the teacher disguise the fact that he may return to certain weaker learners more often than to others; the weaker learners themselves and the others may not readily recognise the teacher's intentions. The disadvantage of random selection is, of course, that it is difficult to ensure that each learner does have a turn to respond; learners at the back of the room are likely to be missed out. This possibility can be counteracted by the mobility of the teacher around the room, as suggested above.

The number of actual responses by the group of learners can be increased very easily by calling upon them all to respond at the same time. The advantage of this 'choral' response is the immediate increase in the number of active responses per learner; the disadvantage is that any fault of an individual learner is usually completely masked by the volume of the choral response. This disadvantage is reduced if quite a number of individual responses precede the choral response; by this procedure, the teacher can satisfy himself that at least a certain proportion of the class will respond accurately, and those learners who had not actually had an opportunity to respond themselves will at least have been exposed to the (correct) stimulus and the (correct or corrected) response a few times already. A choral response does not mean, obviously, the termination of individual responses, and so the teacher may proceed with individual responses afterwards. Another advantage of choral responses is that the whole class participates, thus ensuring the alertness and attention of the whole class. Choral responses are best 'conducted' from the front of the class: the teacher can start this when he returns to the front after moving to and fro in the room. It is difficult to conduct the class from the side of the room or from the middle as the teacher may not be in full view of some of the learners. The teacher can give the stimulus and with a conductor's gesture call forth the choral response. This gesture is to start the class responding at the same time and thus to avoid disharmony. (See Figure 3.)

Figure 3

It is not necessary to give the stimulus every single time the teacher calls upon a learner to respond. If the teacher has said, 'Good morning, Mr Steele' a few times before the imitation procedure actually begins, and he says it for the first half-dozen individual responses, he then often needs only to point and the learner knows what he has to say. The learner has heard that stimulus already at least ten times from the teacher, and half a dozen (correct or corrected) responses from other learners. If the learner stumbles, then, of course, the teacher must give the original stimulus again.

What about the mistakes and stumblings that occur? The teacher must correct or attempt to correct every time. If he wants to establish accurate, fluent pronunciation, he may as well do so right from the beginning. If a learner responds incorrectly, the teacher should either give the whole stimulus again, or give the word or syllable again that was made incorrectly. If two or three attempts still fail to produce an adequate response, it is best for the teacher to leave that learner for a short while, noticing who (and where) he is in order to get him to respond again later. Often, this later response is adequate because the learner's tension has been relieved by being left alone; but it would be as well for that learner to be called upon yet again, later, in order to check and to reinforce the correct version. If however the original mistake persists, the teacher must adopt a different strategy. But he should not continue there and then because under the glare of attention, the learner is likely to tense up. His speech organs also tend to tense up leaving him in a more difficult position than before. The teacher will have to seek out an opportunity to deal with the matter 'privately', perhaps at the end of the lesson or while others are engaged in some other activity. The teacher must put him at his ease and allow him to relax.

If a number of learners make an identical mistake, the teacher should stop the stimulus-response procedure altogether (the rhythm of it will probably have been lost in any case) and he should isolate the offending sound, syllable or word for special attention. The teacher must then decide whether he can deal with the matter quickly enough to return as soon as possible to the main imitation stimulus-response procedure, or whether it is best for him to leave the problem for the time being and persevere with the rest of the dialogue and devote special attention to it on a later occasion.

With a class of 30 learners, 30 identical stimulus/response cycles may prove a bit tedious. Whereas it is our goal for *each* learner to achieve a good pronunciation, we must be careful not to frustrate the effort by tedium. The pace of the procedure is one guard against tedium, and variety is another. So instead of going through 'Good morning, Mr Steele' with all 30 to start off with, it might be as well to take this first utterance of the dialogue first with half the class, interspersed with a couple of choral responses, and then introduce the second item, 'Ah, you're here, Arthur' with the other half. This could lead to alternations of the two stimuli, so that 'Good morning, Mr Steele' is directed to one learner and 'Ah, you're here, Arthur' to the next. The third utterance can then be introduced, 'Yes, I am', and all three utterances can be given as three separate stimuli to different learners. In this way, the teacher can ensure that the half of the class who did not practise 'Good morning, Mr Steele' in individual responses at the beginning of the lesson, will eventually be able to. The ordering of the different stimuli would also help to lift the air of unnaturalness in this drill procedure.

When an imitation procedure is going well, simple substitutions to the text may be added. In the very first dialogue, it may be felt inappropriate to introduce unrehearsed items; but there would be no harm in substituting the teacher's own name, for instance, for 'Mr Steele', or other people's names, including the learners'. This adds not only variety, but even a touch of authenticity.

The teacher must also indicate to the learner whether he is satisfied with the quality of the response, or not. The fact that a teacher repeats the stimulus to one learner is in itself an indication that the teacher was not satisfied. But if he is satisfied, he should indicate that too: by a smile, or a thumbs-up gesture, or a word, or a brief 'OK' or 'Good' (in English). If one response is discernibly superior to a few others preceding it, that too must be acknowledged and praised. Such rewards are important to the learner; they encourage and reassure him and contribute to continuing motivation. A pleasant, generous disposition on the teacher's part makes their learning pleasanter and consequently his own teaching easier. The reward should be given quickly and immediately after a correct response, or even simultaneously with the end of the response when it is obvious that the response is going to be satisfactory. The reward ought not to interfere with the general pace and rhythm of the procedure; there will be opportunities in less intensive, more relaxing activities to give fuller rewards.

The procedure, as described above, is intensive and must not be overdone. When the procedure is going with a swing, it can be exhilarating to both teacher and learners. Consequently, the teacher may be tempted to carry on with a good thing. Initially, 10 minutes may prove to be enough – which may not seem to be very long, but it would be long enough to have had at least 100 responses; if 10 of those had been choral responses, 90 would have been individual, averaging out at 3 individual responses each for 30 learners, which means that each learner actively responded 13 times and was exposed to 10 minutes conducted entirely in the foreign language. (If the mother tongue was used to convey the meaning of the utterances, and was used occasionally to check up on meanings in the course of the 10 minutes' imitation procedure, the overt use of the mother tongue would have accounted for a mere few seconds of the total time – and, incidentally, would have been used by the teacher only, and not by the learners at all. The teacher should also note that this incidental use of the mother tongue does not constitute *practice* in meaning. In this context it is used solely as an aid in pronunciation practice.) Eventually, once the class has been 'trained' in this procedure, or has become used to it, it would be possible to extend the time limit slightly. Furthermore, a teacher must not feel he has failed if he happened not to get through the whole dialogue in the ten minutes or so. After a more relaxing procedure, he may decide to return to the intensive imitation procedure to practise another part of the dialogue. For example, the dialogue under consideration falls into two parts: the first exchange of greetings between *Arthur* and *Mr Steele*, up to 'Yes, I am', and the second exchange between *Arthur* and *Mary*, from 'Good morning, Mary'. 'Yes, I am' may then prove to be a convenient point to discontinue the procedure for a little while.

Let us recap briefly on the essentials of this imitation procedure. The teacher says the utterance a few times; he may convey the meaning by a mother-tongue equivalent, by a visual aid or by depending on context. He begins to point to individuals saying the utterance and getting their response one by one. He moves around the class and when he is conveniently at the front again he calls upon the whole class by conducting a choral response. As each individual responds, or when the whole class responds, he or they imitate the teacher's stimulus without referring in any way to the printed text. While an individual is not directly engaged in an active response, he may glance down at the text and ought, as often as possible, to mouth the words as his colleague speaks his response. The teacher introduces a second utterance, first of all by saying it a few times, and ensuring the learners' understanding, and then proceeds as before with individual and choral responses. Other utterances are introduced in the same way; the series of utterances is then given in sequence, and simple substitutions are introduced too. The teacher rewards satisfactory responses, but repeats his stimulus when a response is unsatisfactory; he then must decide whether he ought to stay with that learner or return to him later or deal with the matter as a separate task. After a while, the teacher reaches the point where he has planned a change of activity, or a change of activity is forced on him by the signs of tiring from the learners.

This is how the imitation procedure might be conducted by the teacher; if it is proceeding rapidly and rhythmically, it is succeeding and is generally very enjoyable. When the imitation procedure comes to an end, a complete change of activity and change of pace are recommended, eg reading, writing, conversation or even drawing, playing or acting. The imitation procedure can be returned to later in the lesson if necessary and desirable.

A brief note now on variations of the original teaching situation given on page 21. The above procedure is valid for groups smaller than 30, but need not be so intensive for small groups of 5 or less. It would be difficult to conduct this procedure with a group much larger than 30, but one obvious strategy to overcome this is to divide the large group into two (or more) smaller groups and conduct the imitation procedure with one group and organise other activities for the other group(s); if an assistant is available, even for part of the time, then he could supervise the other group(s). The procedure is valid for other age groups too; however, with infants who cannot read or who can barely read, there is no point in having the printed version available – in fact it has even been suggested that it is more profitable for them to close their eyes to all external stimuli while the teacher gives the initial listening stimuli.

With eight-year-olds who can read, the printed version could be made available. With the under-fives, such an intensive procedure is quite inappropriate; they are best talked to in the foreign language while they are engaged in other activities. The length of time of the procedure varies with age, too; adults are able and often quite willing to engage in this kind of procedure for longer periods of time than youngsters are. If the group do not share a common mother tongue, then the meaning of items must be conveyed by visual aids (including gestures and acting) or by context. The procedure would be valid for short crash courses too. It is also an open question whether or not this kind of pronunciation practice might not be valuable for those learners who only intend to read the new language; if, as it is often claimed, when we begin to read in our mother tongue we read with a non-vocal internalised form of speech, might it not help in reading in a foreign language to have an equivalent?

2.2 Oral grammar drills

It has been emphasised throughout that the teacher is not concerned with pronunciation only. So, although the teacher may practise dialogues specifically at times for pronunciation, he may well want to use them for practice in grammar, vocabulary and style as well. Grammatical items and features are often practised in oral drill form – substitution exercises, transformation exercises, question and answer sequences and so on. And although the primary intention of the teacher while conducting grammar drills is, of course, grammar, he must also take note of a learner's pronunciation; for instance, if a learner masters the various forms, say, of the past participle, he still has to say them in such a way that a native speaker can recognise them. This need not produce a conflict of intentions. If new material is practised first specifically for pronunciation, then that material is likely to be pronounced satisfactorily when the emphasis shifts to another aspect of language. Pronunciation practice ought normally to precede practice in the other aspects of language for a given set of materials. A new chapter, unit or section is usually devoted to a new grammatical item, a new situation or another language function; if the new material is to be spoken, then it is as well to deal with the pronunciation first in order to devote all the attention afterwards to the new feature. In this way, a conflict of intentions is minimised. If pronunciation is not dealt with first of all, it is possible that a pronunciation matter might interfere with the practice of the new feature, and the teacher has two problems on his hands simultaneously – the new feature and the pronunciation problem.

Such a conflict of intentions can be resolved also by confining observations on pronunciation during oral drills to incidental remarks. The new feature may have been reproduced in a learner's response to a stimulus, but with poor pronunciation. The learner should then be expected to give the response again with correct pronunciation. Accuracy in pronunciation can be expected from the first day, and if it is, it can be expected subsequently in all oral work. Fluency of pronunciation can also be expected from the first day, and can be expected in all subsequent oral work which requires whole utterances and not just isolated words. A teacher must, however, use his discretion. If a learner is having a problem with the newly introduced feature, then the teacher may have temporarily to turn a deaf ear to a pronunciation mistake, for the sake of concentrating on the other feature. He ought, nevertheless, to encourage satisfactory pronunciation immediately afterwards, or, taking note of the learner, at a convenient time later.

In the majority of cases an individual learner's pronunciation problem in oral drilling can be dealt with in this incidental way. The teacher's main objective is the practice of whatever material is contained in the oral drill. If many learners reproduce a similar problem in their pronunciation in the drill, then the teacher must concede that previous pronunciation practice was inadequate, and he may well have to revert to an imitation procedure just to get the matter under control. The teacher is in charge, not a set of guidelines or a methodology, and he must feel free to switch his tactics to suit a new and possibly unexpected set of circumstances.

With the kind of materials we have considered so far (*Starting Out*), the teacher might well follow through a set of objectives for a chapter and then repeat them in the next chapter. His objectives may well include pronunciation practice, grammar practice, vocabulary exercises, comprehension questions, spontaneous and independent conversation and so forth for that one chapter. As that chapter is completed, he might well adopt the same set of objectives for the next chapter, starting again with pronunciation practice, and then grammar practice and the rest. This set of objectives becomes cyclical in operation, and in this way, no one aspect is neglected. This is particularly important in the initial stages of language practice.

2.3 Intermediate and advanced students

When learners reach an intermediate or advanced level, their articulation of consonants and vowels and their production of word accent and rhythm should have been well consolidated, if pronunciation has been practised intensively and remarked on incidentally but consistently, and if accuracy and fluency have been expected constantly. Certain intonation forms should also have been consolidated.

What one finds, however, in very many cases at an intermediate or advanced level, is a learner who in other respects – knowledge of grammar, reading comprehension, independent writing, translation – has clearly reached that level, but has failed to do so in pronunciation. What may well be needed is a 'dose' of the intensive imitation procedure described above, punctuated with appropriate attention to specific problems in isolation.

Let us take another language-teaching situation with another coursebook, to describe what procedures we might adopt. Imagine a group of 15 learners whose ages range from 16 to 60 and whose national backgrounds vary enormously too. Their course is being held in Britain (or in any other native English-speaking environment) and the teacher is a native English speaker, who happens to know one of the learners' mother tongues, but one only. The learners' previous language learning has been very varied too; some have been taught wholly by a direct method, others by an audio-lingual method and others again by the traditional grammar-translation method. Their purposes in improving their English are also very varied. Some are students, others are housewives, waiters, au pairs, and so on. What follows would apply to either evening classes or more intensive crash or summer vacation courses. For a coursebook we might take *Freeway: English for short courses*. There is less obvious attention to pronunciation intended by the author than there would be for a beginners' course; nevertheless, one of the basic aims is practice in speaking: 'by the end of the course all the students should feel that their ability to understand native speakers, sustain a conversation ... has increased'. (Ttofi 1978: 4)

Unit 1 contains reading material, short illustrative dialogues, illustrations, grammar exercises, reading comprehension, composition outlines and supplementary exercises. The initial structures to be practised are:

A   She's obviously bored.
    She seems to be bored.
    It looks as if she's bored.

B   They're obviously having an argument.
    They seem to be having an argument.
    It looks as if they're having an argument.

C   He seems to have fallen asleep.
    It looks as if he's fallen asleep.
    He seems to have fallen asleep while he was reading his newspaper.
    It looks as if he fell asleep while he was reading his newspaper.

(A, B and C refer to different levels of ability. The author's intention is that the above sentences should provide a model for subsequent responses in a dialogue. The three sentences for A are the variations in responses that the teacher is to expect; similarly, variations for B and C are given. Each variation is to be practised.)

The teacher will no doubt get some idea of the variety of pronunciation abilities in the group of learners from his initial contact and greetings. He will note, mentally, those that will obviously need a great deal of pronunciation practice and those that will not need as much. At some point in the first lesson or two, he will want to start using the course book material. The learners will enjoy the illustrations and theme of Unit 1 ('cartoon humour'), and eventually they will move on to the short dialogues. The sentences of A and similar ones with the same structures will have been used in the initial conversation about the first cartoon. The first dialogue accompanies the next cartoon, and the comment 'She's obviously bored' is required.

The teacher can adopt an approach here that is identical to the fast intensive stimulus-response imitation procedure described for beginners. The teacher gives the utterance 'She's obviously bored' a couple of times, pointing to the character in the cartoon. Reference to a mother-tongue equivalent is now, of course, impossible, except for the odd learner or two whose mother tongue is known by the teacher. It should obviously not become a regular feature to give the mother-tongue equivalent to a privileged one or two learners; if, however, one of them is in serious difficulties, then the teacher should not hesitate to use the mother tongue occasionally. Jealousy of such a privilege is not aroused if its use is kept to a minimum, and if the general atmosphere in the group is relaxed and the rapport between teacher and learner and between the learners themselves is good. Glancing at the printed version should be encouraged, except when the learner is actively responding; responses should not just be read off, since the primary stimulus is the teacher's spoken one. The teacher should practise the first comment with about half of the class and then introduce 'She seems to be bored' for variety, and eventually introduce 'It looks as if she's bored' as well. All three can then be practised together. The teacher must also point to the character in the cartoon as the new comments are introduced so that the learners will realise that they all mean the same thing in that context.

As for beginners, the teacher can select learners at random, by pointing to them to give the responses; he can move around the room and occasionally conduct choral responses. The teacher should only be satisfied with responses that are both accurate and fluent. This is preparation for spontaneous and independent conversation, where contributions to the conversation need to be fluent and easily understood. Mouthing could be encouraged too, to make listening time more productive. This procedure with three short sentences should only take a few minutes.

The next move is controlled by the items that follow in the

dialogue. A cue is given in the textbook that should call forth 'He's obviously more interested in watching the programme'. The teacher could point to the character in the cartoon to confirm a correct association with the context. Similar comments based on the model sentences of A will yield 'He seems to be more interested . . .' and 'It looks as if he's more interested . . .' which should be introduced, as above. Then the three original comments about *her* and the new ones about *him* could be interwoven, and in this way, the unnaturalness of the procedure can be relieved. The imitation procedure should not last long. If the learners are already acquainted with it, they will cope with it effortlessly: if they are not, the whole procedure of the six comments in their three varied forms that form the dialogue may be split up into two short sessions of ten minutes.

3 Accuracy

In the next three chapters, we shall look in detail at specific problems in teaching English pronunciation. The main aim is a degree of accuracy and fluency that is appropriate to the level of intelligibility that the teacher has set for his learners. (If you have any difficulty with the terminology used in these chapters, please consult the Glossary of phonetic terms, page 120.)

Accuracy is required in every aspect of language: consistently inaccurate spelling impairs readability, for instance; inaccuracy in the form of words and the structure of clauses and sentences, incorrect choice of vocabulary, incorrect choice of style all contribute to the distortion of communication. But nothing distorts like inaccurate articulation.

Accuracy ought to be sought after right from the very beginning. Accuracy does not grow mysteriously with the passing of time and nor does it grow out of vague and fuzzy approximations. Conscious effort is required on the part of the learner until new articulatory habits are formed. And the best time to start is right at the beginning, for two reasons: firstly, the sooner the right habits are established, the better; and secondly, later remedial work is a burdensome task and could have been avoided by insisting on hard work at first. In later stages of language learning, emphasis should be upon developing independent spontaneous communication by the learner, preferably unhampered by difficulties of a low-level kind like pronunciation.

The basic strategy is *imitation*, as outlined in the previous chapter. The teacher should accept as correct only those responses that are made with satisfactory articulation of the consonants and vowels, satisfactory word accent and rhythm, satisfactory intonation, all at a satisfactory rate of delivery. If the accent is misplaced or the rhythm inaccurate or jerky, then tapping or stabbing the air with the finger is usually an effective way of correcting; if the intonation is inaccurate, a flowing gesture of the hand or nodding of the head or a chalk line on the blackboard usually is sufficient. If the utterance is slowed down to highlight a particular point, then it must be speeded up again afterwards. If a consonant or vowel is at fault, then a variety of techniques can be employed.

3.1 Demonstration, association and explanation

The teacher should isolate the sound. With the first dialogue we considered in the last chapter, the /θ/ of *Arthur* might prove troublesome. The most obvious technique is *demonstration*: in this case by exaggerating the articulation, by pushing the tongue out between the teeth further than is usual. The learners can imitate individually and/or chorally. Then the accented vowel /ɑ/ can be added, thus /ɑθ/, with less obvious tongue protrusion, and the learners imitate that. Then /ə/ is added to make /ɑθə/, which again is imitated. And finally the whole utterance is given again, first of all slowing up a little over *Arthur* but eventually increasing to a normal rate of delivery. Once attention is off the /θ/, it is almost inevitable that some will slip back into their previous mis-articulation. The teacher should simply call their attention to their slip, and if need be, go quickly through the procedure again. Again, almost inevitably, some will misarticulate in the next lesson, but once the initial basic steps of demonstration have been given, getting learners to articulate a particular sound correctly speeds up. Patience is a virtue every teacher must acquire.

/p, b, m, f, v, θ, ð, w/ are all very easily demonstrable, but, of course, every sound can be produced in isolation, to be imitated. It is also often a good idea to highlight the difference between the English sound and the nearest equivalent in the learner's mother tongue; if that is not possible, the teacher must take note of the learner's misarticulation and reproduce it in order to contrast it with the English form. This may well mean that the teacher must contrast English /θ/ with the [s] of some speakers, the [f] of others, and the dental version [t̪] of others again. If the learner produces a sound that corresponds with another English phoneme, the teacher could give the meanings of the mis-articulation if an actual word in English is produced, eg 'If you say [sɪŋ] instead of /θɪŋ/, that means . . . (whatever *sing* is, in the mother tongue)'.

If demonstration is not feasible, *association* may be. If the /g/ of *Good* proves difficult, the sound must be isolated, and attention can be drawn to its similarities with /b, d/ on account of voicing and muscular tension, and with /k/ on account of its point of articulation. The same step-by-step building-up procedure then follows, until 'Good morning' is produced. The voicing of /v, ð, z, ʒ/ can be pointed out by associating /v/ with /f/, etc, alternating each by switching voice on and off; voice can be heard clearly by cupping hands over ears, and can be felt by pressing a finger against the Adam's apple. /ŋ/ can be associated with /m, n/ and with /k, g/. /w/ can be associated with /u/, /j/ with /i/, and /r/ with /ʒ/. Again, as above, it is often a good idea to draw the learner's attention to the meanings of words unintentionally produced, eg if *berry* is produced for *very*, then giving the meaning of *berry* highlights the importance of getting /v/ articulated correctly. The /v/ can be associated with /f/ and practised with voice; then /e/ and /rɪ/ are added.

If association is not feasible, then *explanation* may be. It might be best with some learners to add explanation to demonstration and association. /r/, where the tip of the tongue must be curled up and back, can be explained as follows: 'Start with [ɑ]; curl the tongue tip up and backwards, so that the tip is pointing inwards. Hold it there; prolong the sound. Make yourself conscious of the position of the tongue; keep the tongue fixed and "switch off" voice; while keeping the tongue fixed, switch voice back on and off, producing /r . . . r . . . r/'. If need be, do the process again, but more quickly. Then try and produce the /r/ without starting from [ɑ]. Follow the /r/ with a vowel like /i/ or /ɪ/. Do it again and say /ri/. Try *Mary* slowly as /meːəri/ and then more quickly as /ˈmeəri/ or /ˈmeərɪ/. Try *restaurant* slowly as /re-stə-rənt/ and then more quickly as /ˈrestərənt/. (*Mary* occurs in the dialogue of Chapter 1 of *Access to English: Starting out* (see page 23), and *restaurant* in the reading material, which no doubt will be practised orally as well.) Explanations are given, naturally, in the learner's mother tongue if he is a beginner, but in English with intermediate and advanced learners who require such remedial work. Explanations can be supplemented by diagrams on the blackboard or in printed material, if available. If the teacher is not in a position to use a learner's mother tongue, then of course he must resort to diagrams.

3.2 Discrimination

If the problem is one of perception – the learner does not seem able to perceive the difference between a set of sounds – then the isolated sounds must be patiently contrasted. One set of vowels that often produces problems is /ɑ, ɒ, ɔ/. Vowel length is significant here, and the shortness of /ɒ/ may be the only distinguishing factor that a learner can latch on to at first. To distinguish /ɑ/ and /ɔ/, lip rounding may be the key factor. The fact that the learner does not depend on changes of actual vowel quality (the positioning of the tongue) is not important. The fact that he can now distinguish the three vowels by some crude device is sufficient at first – that, after all, represents a new awareness, a new perception for him. That now has to be reinforced. The simplest first step is some form of discrimination procedure: the learner indicates, on paper or by pointing, for instance, that he perceives a particular articulation as one or another vowel. Then two articulations are given, and the learner must decide whether they are identical or not. One or two simple words may then be introduced; especially useful are minimal pairs like *heart* and *hot*, *pot* and *port*, *card* and *cod*, and *cod* and *cord*. Visuals might be associated with these, and the learner must choose the appropriate visual. Nonsense words are easier to devise, but have the obvious disadvantage of being meaningless; nevertheless they can be helpful in developing discrimination. At a slightly later stage, words (or even nonsense items) can be simply dictated, and discrimination is assessed by correct identification of the word or item dictated; perfect spelling is not the criterion here, but correct identification of the word.

This ear-training practice needs to be followed up with articulation practice, accompanied if necessary by demonstration, association, explanation and visual aid. Most learners, most of the time, can perceive contrasts in the pronunciation system, simply by demonstration; but in those cases where a learner cannot, some kind of ear-training practice, as described above, has to precede articulation practice, because faulty perception leads to faulty articulation. Articulation practice needs to start off with the consonant or vowel practised in isolation; the learner has to imitate the teacher saying /θ ... θ .../, /ʒ ... ʒ .../ or /ʌ ... ʌ .../ and so on. Then the consonant must be combined with a vowel, and the vowel with a consonant. Then a word must be built up, and finally, the word must be incorporated into a meaningful phrase. The teacher should persevere with this step-by-step approach to articulation practice until the learner can say the phrase without undue hesitation over the difficult sound. The teacher's aim eventually is to get the learner to say things without conscious effort in articulation. Pronunciation is not an end in itself, but only a means, and that is why it is essential to progress beyond practising sounds in single words (unless they are typical single-word utterances like 'Stop!', 'Quick!', 'Marvellous!') and practise making meaningful utterances.

We are now in a position to consider techniques for each of the English consonants and vowels. These techniques are only necessary if straightforward demonstration and association fail. It is useful to try and highlight the error by contrasting the misarticulation with the accepted standard forms, or by contrasting the standard form with the nearest equivalent in the learner's mother tongue: 'Careful now, it's *x* not *y*. Listen again; can you hear the difference: *x, x, x* and *y, y, y*. Now, try it again: *x* (pause) . . .'. Another note of caution: except with advanced students and linguistically trained students, do not attempt to use phonetics jargon in a serious way. Terms like 'voiced' and 'voiceless' might be useful, but it is perfectly possible to 'translate' phonetics jargon into ordinary language. We are not training prospective phoneticians. *Voice*, for example, can be referred to as the 'buzzing sound made in the throat' (see page 49).

It is also useful to follow up instruction in class by recommending learners to memorise sentences containing a liberal sprinkling of difficult sounds, for private study or homework. The teacher himself must decide when he can confidently recommend such memorisation; if he does so too early, then the likelihood is that he will be encouraging consolidation of faulty pronunciation.

3.3 Stops

Many learners produce /p, t, k/ in such a way that they resemble /b, d, g/ too closely, and the reason for this is their lack of aspiration. It is true that /p, t, k/ are not aspirated after a syllable-initial /s/, but then no contrast between them and /b, d, g/ occurs there. Let us take /k/ to represent the voiceless fortis stops in this respect. Articulate /k/ in complete isolation, with no vowel following, not even [ə]: the result is [kʰ]; get the learner to imitate. Make him aware of the 'puff of air' that follows, by getting him to feel it on the back of his hand in front of his mouth, or by holding a thin piece of paper in front of his lips (it should be blown over). Another way is to get him to notice the effect of this puff of air on a lighted match held close to his lips – but I would not recommend a class of 30 eleven-year-olds to do that! (See Figure 4.) When he is conscious of this puff of air, articulate the [kʰ] as before and add a vowel, but delay the addition of the vowel so that the aspiration is prolonged; get the learner to imitate, and then to reproduce the sequence a few times independently. After a few attempts, he should be able to do it satisfactorily; then he must shorten the delay of the following vowel until he can produce an item (either a nonsense item, or an actual English word) acceptably. He must eventually be able to produce [kʰ] in a word that he is learning or in a meaningful utterance, eg *Careful! Can I go?* Aspiration of /p/ and /t/ can be practised in the same way. /k/ should also be practised before /l, r, w, j/; the same technique can be adopted, with, say, the /l/ being delayed, thus [kʰl]; the delay must then be shortened and eliminated, so that the aspiration is heard in the /l/ itself. This goes for /k/ with /r, w, j/ also, and similarly for /p/ and /t/.

If the learner possesses no equivalent of one of the voiceless fortis stops, /p/ for instance, the same technique can be followed.

It is as well to remember that all stops at the end of a syllable are unreleased if another consonant follows immediately; for example /p/ in [ˈkʰæptʰɪn] *captain* rather than [ˈkʰæpʰtʰɪn]. The teacher should simply demonstrate how the lips are kept closed while the /t/ is formed; with /k/ in *action* [ˈækʃən] (not [ˈækʰʃən]), the back of the tongue is held against the soft palate while the next consonant is formed. However there is no need to insist on /t/

and he may not be distinguishing ... speech ... do more practise
and [bædə] at first, since ... [æ] out final [æ]
product branching. Pronounce ... say [bæd], and help
lengthy at [d]. It is said ... vowels ... to remember that
a vowel used on [d] ... final ... d] is longer than
preceding a final [t] ... the initial [t] ... may be get so
it may produce a ... as in length of ... vowel used in
[t] final.

3.6 Nasal

... there ... nasal ... problem ... with /m, n,
... they are usually pronounced ... final position than
... in final position. If a learner produces the nasal
... may sound ... it is a sudden mishandling ... afraid be th
... this ... however much type all learner errors.

Figure 4

being formed at the alveolar ridge in a phrase like *not those*, since so many English speakers produce a glottal stop [ʔ] there: [nɒʔðəuz].

If the learner possesses no equivalent of one or all of the voiced lenis set /b, d, g/, then he has to learn to add the voicing feature One technique is to make him aware of the voicelessness of /p, t, k/ first; if the teacher says a word or an item with /p/ between long vowels like [ɑːpʰɑː] and gets the learner to imitate him with hands clapped over ears, the learner should be able to hear an interruption to the buzzing of voice during the articulation of the /p/. Now demonstrate the same kind of thing with /b/, getting the learner to try and maintain the buzzing while he closes and opens his lips. Get him to do this until he can produce [ɑːbɑː] without much effort. The preceding vowel must then be reduced to a very short vowel, and perhaps changed to [ə]; the accent must fall on the [bɑ], as [əˈbɑ]. The learner must practise until the initial vowel is lost altogether. This technique applies to /d/ and /g/ too.

A learner may be able to produce /b, d, g/ satisfactorily in most positions in a word, but not, perhaps, at the end: the words *bat* and *bad* may not be distinguished in his speech. He must practise *bad* as [bædə] at first and go on practising until that final [ə] is reduced to nothing. Pretend to be about to say [bædə] and halt abruptly at [d]. It is also helpful for the teacher to remember that a vowel, nasal or /l/ preceding a final /b, d, g/ is longer than preceding a final /p, t, k/. So a partial solution may be to get a learner to make a conscious effort to lengthen the vowel, nasal or /l/ a little.

3.4 Nasals

There are not usually a great number of problems with /m, n, ŋ/. In English they are usually somewhat longer in final position than they are in initial position. If a learner produces the nasals of *sum*, *sun* and *sung* too short, it is not a serious mistake; and if need be, it can be easily overcome by drawing the learner's attention to their length in native English and by demonstration. If the teacher feels that it *must* be overcome, he must get the learner to practise words in isolation and then in longer meaningful utterances.

A greater problem is the total lack of a final nasal. This can be practised by starting off with the nasal between vowels, [ɑnɑ], placing the accent on the first syllable ['ɑnɑ], and gradually reducing the final vowel to a rapid [ə] before eliminating it altogether. If nasalisation of the preceding vowel creeps in, this will not matter as such nasalisation (if it is not *too* noticeable) is typical of most native English speech.

3.5 Fricatives

Introductory practice of /θ/, and, by implication, /ð/ singly and in consonant clusters has already been touched on (pages 43 and 46). /f/ and /v/ can be demonstrated in a similar way. /s/ does not usually present a problem unless the learner produces it as a dental sound, in which case it may occasionally be mistaken for a learner's misarticulation of /θ/. Such a learner must be guided to press the tongue up high against the upper gum. If /z/ is a problem, it can usually be associated with the articulation of /s/. Voicing is the usual difficulty, however, and the procedure adopted for /b/ above (page 49) is valid in this case too. Start off with [ɑːsɑː] with hands cupped over ears to detect the interruption of the buzzing of voice for [s]; demonstrate the same kind of thing, trying to maintain the buzzing while pressing the tongue against the upper gum as for [s]. Get the learner to do this until he can produce [ɑːzɑː] without much effort. Make sure the accent is on the second syllable and gradually reduce the first vowel to [ə]: [əˈzɑː], and finally eliminate [ə] altogether. To practise it in final position, move the accent to the first syllable and gradually reduce the following vowel to [ə], thus [ˈɑːzə], before finally eliminating [ə]. The voicing of /v, ð, ʒ/ can be practised in the same way; remember that there is no need to practise /ʒ/ in initial position. Note, too, that /v, ð, z, ʒ/ are noticeably shorter than /f, θ, s, ʃ/, especially at the end of a word, and that the vowel preceding them is noticeably longer than it is before these voiceless fricatives.

With /s, z/ it is not useful to refer learners to the grooving of the tongue; the groove is limited to the tip and blade of the tongue and appears to be too short for many people to appreciate. The groove for /ʃ, ʒ/ is longer and broader as it extends from the tip and blade over the (so-called) front of the tongue and is more easily felt kinaesthetically. The position of the tongue for /ʃ, ʒ/ can be associated quite easily with the tongue's position for /i/ or /j/; in fact, there is even a kind of grooving for /i/ and /j/ since the sides of the tongue are quite firmly pressed against the upper back teeth. The difference between the position for /ʃ, ʒ/ and /i, j/ can be demonstrated by making a series of long /i/ and long /ʃ/ combined, thus /iːʃːiːʃːiːʃ . . ./. It should be noticed that the sides of the tongue remain firmly pressed against the upper back teeth for both /i/ and /ʃ/, but that the tongue 'rocks' up and down. With

/i/, the blade of the tongue is low, and the body of the tongue is quite high; with /ʃ/, the blade is raised, and the body lowered. This rocking, with the sides of the tongue fixed and acting as the fulcrum, can be felt with a series of /iːʃː/. Notice too that the lips round slightly for /ʃ/ and spread for /iː/. Once a learner can perform the /iːʃː/ sequence, it will be necessary to add another vowel immediately after the /ʃ/; then the accent is shifted to the second syllable: /iːˈʃɑ/; then /iː/ is reduced and eliminated, leaving /ʃɑ/. Words with /ʃ/ are then built up and included in meaningful utterances. In practising /ʃr-/ it may be necessary to allow [ə] to intervene at first, before it is reduced and finally eliminated. For /ʃ/ in final position, it has already been established after /i/; it is then best practised with front vowels (/ɪ, e, æ/) before practice with other vowels, diphthongs and /l/. /ʒ/ can be introduced in the same way.

The articulation of /h/ can be related to whispering as /h/ is a voiceless vowel sound. It could therefore be introduced in whispered speech, and particularly in 'whispered laughter'; in the latter case, change the vowel quality of the laughter, eg from [hɑhɑhɑ] to [hihihi] to [huhuhu] and so on. Isolate one sequence of, say, [hi], lengthen the [h] and voice the vowel, as [hːi], and practise with other vowels too. Reduce the length of [h] eventually to normal proportions. Another technique is to get the students to imagine that they are breathing heavily on to glass (eg mirror or window) to leave vapour on it. This heavy (voiceless) breathing is simply a strongly articulated [h]. Try it with varying vowel qualities, at first keeping the [h] long. Try it in other nonsense items and English words, and then reduce the length of [h] to normal proportions.

3.6 Affricates

If /ʃ, ʒ/ are no problem, /tʃ, dʒ/ are usually not a problem either. If they are, however, then the tongue position can be practised as for /ʃ/ above, as it is practically identical; the rocking motion is the same, but as the tongue rocks into the [ʃ] position, the blade must be raised to the point where the hard palate begins to rise steeply behind the alveolar ridge, and the blade must actually stop the flow of air momentarily. The technique then proceeds as for /ʃ/ above.

The voicing of /dʒ/ can be practised and established in the same way as for /b, d, g/ (page 49) and the voiced fricatives (page 50).

3.7 Laterals and approximants

/l/ presents all kinds of problems, serious and not so serious. In many languages, the English /l/ has no equivalent as a separate independent phoneme; it may occur as an allophone of another phoneme (usually of some kind of /r/) or it simply does not occur at all; in either case, lateralness is not perceived or felt. The teacher must persevere with demonstration and explanation. This is one of those cases where it is absolutely vital for the learner to be put at his ease, and relax. Start with [ə] and encourage, by demonstration and the learner's imitating, the raising of the tip of the tongue to the alveolar ridge – only the tip, not the body of the tongue or else some kind of [d] is likely. Persevere, and encourage the learner to persevere! When he produces something like [əl], get him to prolong the [l], thus [əl:]. Produce a long [l] for him punctuated by glottal stops, thus [lʔlʔlʔ], and get him to produce [əlʔlʔlʔl] with conscious attention to the position of the tongue for [l] so that the tongue remains fixed through the glottal stops as well. Get him to produce the same sequence with longer intervals between the glottal stops, and get him to try and accentuate each long [l]; [ə'l:ʔ'l:ʔ'l:ʔ'l]. The next step is to insert a vowel before the glottal stops, thus [ə'l:ʔ'l:ʔ'l:ʔ'l:] and then get him to produce one single sequence [ə'l:ɑʔ]. Practise single sequences like this, gradually reducing and finally eliminating [ə], thus [l:ɑ'ʔ] Now the learner must practise this long [l] before other vowels in nonsense items and in actual words, eg [lɒŋ] for *long*. With further practice, this long [l] can be reduced to normal length.

Other learners produce /l/ dentally; this is not a serious problem as [l̪] cannot be mistaken for anything else in the English pronunciation system. Such learners must be guided, if it is desired, to press the tip and blade against the upper gum.

Many learners make no distinction between the clear and dark varieties of English /l/. This rarely leads to any difficulty or ambiguity in interpretation; a clear [l] for a dark one in *till eight* may lead to its interpretation as *till late*, but such cases are rarely problematical. The teacher may well feel content with one [l] articulation in all positions; many English speakers do not use a dark [l] (although the majority do), and many American speakers do not use a clear [l].

An explanation of the articulation of initial /r/ appeared on page 44. Many learners produce the variety of /r/ that occurs in their mother tongue; a teacher must decide whether to be content with that, or not. A lingual roll is probably more acceptable to most native speakers than any uvular articulation; a lingual tap is more acceptable again, as it occurs in native speech regularly after /θ, ð/ and often between vowels, eg in *very, sorry, hurry*.

The main problem with /w/ is distinguishing it from /v/. It should be associated with the vowel /u/, drawing attention to the strongly rounded lips, very much in the shape for whistling. The /w/ of a word like *wet* can be lengthened into a [u:], but maintaining the accent on /e/, thus [u:ˈetʰ]. Gradually reduce the length of [u:] to [w], making sure that the rounding of the lips is maintained, that the lower lip does not slip back to articulate with the upper teeth, and that no friction is caused. Remember too that preceding consonants are also rounded, thus /k/ in *quite*, /t/ in *twelve*, etc. For those learners who confuse /w/ with /v/, partly because of a spelling difficulty, they should be allowed no recourse to printed material while their attention is focused on this particular matter. This may well mean that this pronunciation problem should be dealt with quite separately from the kind of practice discussed previously in the imitation procedure (see page 27).

Problems with /j/ can be dealt with similarly. /j/ should be associated with /i/, and produced at first as [i:] in a word like *yes*, thus [i:'es], with the accent on the [e]. Gradually reduce the length of [i:] to [j], making sure that no friction is allowed to creep in. Some learners confuse /j/ with /dʒ/ on account of spelling; as for the /w/ – /v/ problem above, it would be as well if practice of /j/ for such learners was kept quite separate from the regular practice in the imitation procedure.

3.8 Vowels and diphthongs

It is difficult to treat the vowels in the same way as most of the consonants. The classification of consonants depends very much on identifying the articulator involved, the point of articulation and the degree of interference; and similarly, explanations of how to articulate consonants depend very much on the learner's ability to *feel* articulations physically with the lips and tongue. Vowels have practically no tongue contact and a learner will not readily understand instructions to raise the tongue slightly or to retract it slightly without some degree of phonetics training. But, again, we are not training phoneticians. Hence, we have to rely more on auditory control than on articulatory control in dealing with the vowels.

Nevertheless, there are three factors that we can describe: length of the vowel, jaw opening and tongue movement; lip rounding is a fourth, but less important, factor. With a vowel system of 20 units – which is fairly rich compared to the vowel systems of a very large number of languages – contrasting two or three vowels and/or diphthongs is crucial. The division of vowels into long and short has been dealt with elsewhere (page 9): it is vital to maintain the length difference to make up for any difficulty in reaching quality differences. Not that the latter should be neglected, but it is a common observation that quality differences are more difficult to achieve than length differences. A crude device for trying to achieve quality differences is to refer to jaw opening. Now, it *is* possible to articulate all the English vowels and diphthongs with strongly clenched jaws, but native English speakers do not usually do so! So, although jaw opening is secondary to tongue height, it nevertheless can be used quite effectively. Thus the difference between /i/ and /ɪ/, for instance, can be demonstrated with reference to the degree of jaw opening as well as length. Tongue movement is obviously important in demonstrating diphthongs. A diphthong like /ɑɪ/ can be demonstrated and followed up with reference to the considerable movement of the tongue. (This movement of the tongue is, of course, accompanied by movement of the jaw.) Lip rounding is occasionally of some consequence, especially in distinguishing /ɔ/ from /ɑ, ʌ, ɜ/.

The main techniques in establishing acceptable vowel production are ear training to establish the perception of contrasts, and imitation. There is plenty of material published that the teacher can use to supplement his main materials and any materials he has devised himself (see Materials for pronunciation practice, page 113). Such material consists mainly of words grouped for contrastive purposes, and sentences and whole stories liberally seeded with a particular sound; there are also rhymes and ditties, references to spelling, and games and such like.

Here are some examples:

1 Are these the same or different:

   a pitch   pitch?
   b peach   pitch?
   c pitch   peach?

The teacher says each pair of items, and the learner has to indicate whether he hears any difference between them. He can do this by raising a hand if he hears them as different and by keeping his hand down if he hears them as the same. Or he can write his response down by putting a √ by the letters *a*, *b* and *c* if he hears them as the same, or an × if he hears them as different; alternatively, he can write S for *same* and D for *different*. In some workbooks, the learner has to ring or underline <u>same</u> or <u>different</u> as he hears them, eg:

a	same	different
b	same	different
c	same	different

2 Which one is different:

pitch	peach	pitch?
sheep	ship	ship?
cheek	cheek	chick?

A similar procedure to 1 can be adopted. Alternatively, a learner may call out 'First', 'Second', 'Third' to indicate which word was different.

The same can be done with sentences, too, eg:

The little boy beat his sister.	I am leaving with my brother.
beat	living
bit	leaving

3 Here are two/three words written down (or, two/three pictures). Point to the right one when I say a word (or, write down either A, B, C, etc):

cart	cot	
part	pot	port
bus	boss	
cot	coat	

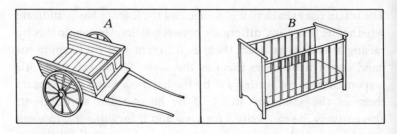

4 Imitation of single words, phrases and sentences, as for example, Figure 5 from Trim 1975: 13.

5 Recitation of longer passages, such as the following from Mackenzie 1967: p.10f, (intended to practise /æ/):

A man sat on a black cat and the black cat was squashed flat, for the man was a fat man. 'Oh, that fat man is a bad man,' said the black cat, 'he's squashed me flat and that makes me sad.' The black cat had only a thin little voice, of course, for he was a flat cat and you should know that a flat cat's voice is à thin flat voice. But the fat man heard what the sad black cat said, and he said, the man said, 'Oh, flat black cat I am sad! I thought you were a black mat, and that's why I sat where I sat.' 'I wish you hadn't sat where you sat,' said the cat. 'It was sitting where you sat that squashed me flat, as flat as a flat black mat.' 'That's bad,' said the fat man, 'very bad. Wouldn't you be glad if I hadn't sat where I sat?' 'Yes,' said the cat, 'for you're fat, too fat for this sad black cat on whom you've sat. Can't you stand up, fat man?' 'Yes, I can,' said the man, and he did stand up. 'That makes me glad,' said the black cat, 'very glad.' And the cat and the cat's voice grew fatter and fatter and gladder and gladder. Then the black cat, who had been a flat, flat cat, grew fat, quite fat again, but not of course as fat as the fat man who had sat on the latterly sad fat cat. 'I'm sorry I sat on you, you poor black cat,' said the man, 'come and sit on my lap.' So the black cat sat on the man's lap and the man and the cat were glad and sang sad bad mad songs to each other, and that was that.

a pet
ə 'pet

a pat
ə 'pæt

one man
'wʌn 'mæn

many men
'menɪ 'men

a net
ə 'net

a gnat
ə 'næt

pedalling
'pedlɪŋ

paddling
'pædlɪŋ

Ted | has Dad's hat | on his head |
'ted | hæz 'dædz 'hæt | ɔn ɪz ˌhed |

Jack has a check
cap | in his hand |
'dʒæk hæz ə 'tʃek
'kæp ɪn ɪz 'hænd |

Jack's Czech friend | Franz |
is very expansive |
dʒæks 'tʃek 'frend | 'frænts |
ɪz 'verɪ ɪk'spænsɪv |

Franz's French friend |
is very expensive |
'fræntsɪz | 'frentʃ | 'frend |
ɪz 'verɪ ɪks'pensɪv |

Figure 5 Trim 1975.

6 For rhymes, songs and games, see Dakin 1971 (this includes an index of songs and rhymes for particular pronunciation problems), Dorry 1966, Jordon & Mackay 1976, Lee 1979, and Trim 1978.*

---

* There is a further book in this series, by Shelagh Rixon, which deals with games in the language classroom.

4 Fluency

Fluency is the smooth joining-up of elements at an acceptable speed of delivery. Like accuracy and other notions in language learning, it relates not only to pronunciation, but to other aspects of language as well, including grammar, selection of appropriate vocabulary, style and discourse. Having to work out correct grammatical forms in the middle of an utterance disturbs fluency, as does searching in the mind for the right word. Similarly, writing needs to be fluent as well as speech; fluency is relevant for interpretation, for example, as well as expressing oneself in conversation. Nevertheless, we are here primarily concerned with fluency of pronunciation

The general definition of fluency already given can now be applied to pronunciation specifically. Fluent pronunciation is the smooth joining of phonemes and larger elements at an acceptable speed of delivery. We cannot define fluency any more directly than this because native speakers of a language (or a dialect) will be regarded, on the whole, as fluent speakers of that language (or dialect), despite the range of average speeds for different individuals and despite the range of different speeds for any given individual in different sets of circumstances. For instance, a native speaker of English will vary in speeds of delivery on account of his physical condition – it is less easy to be fluent when you are tired; and on account of his emotional condition – embarrassment, for instance, impairs general fluency, and so does fear, and some events leave us totally speechless! The subject matter affects fluency too; the less familiar we are with the subject that we are dealing with, the less fluent we become. So, although we would wish to regard native speakers as naturally fluent, there is a wide range of degree of fluency amongst them.

We need not, therefore, expect an extremely elegant fluency from language learners. Nevertheless, what we as teachers can aim to do is to practise pronunciation in such a way that knowledge of and articulatory ability in the language itself should not be the main obstacles to fluency. It is obvious, for example, that we could not expect a language learner to be more fluent when he is embarrassed than a native speaker would be; nor to be more fluent when dealing with an unfamiliar matter than a native speaker would be. Fluency is relative to a number of factors, as suggested above.

Fluency is important for the person being spoken to, in the same way as accuracy is. Lack of fluency, like lack of accuracy, can place quite a strain on the listener. If pronunciation is very jerky, this will mean that the listener will have to listen very carefully and will not be able to relax; in other words, he has to work hard at what he receives. This will eventually have the effect that the listener will not wish to receive what the speaker wants to say.

Hesitation and pauses do not necessarily indicate a breakdown of fluency. Hesitation is a common feature of native speech, as we search in our minds for just the right word we need, or as we decide to stop or rephrase entirely what we want to say. A language learner must be expected to do the same kind of thing. Pauses have definite linguistic functions; and (in the right place) are marks of competent speech.

Fluency also indicates that the speaker is using linguistic elements with a minimum of effort, and with a minimum of conscious decision taking. This comes as the result of practice.

It should be clear, then, that fluency is not simply a matter of speed, as one might presume. But nevertheless, speed is one of the factors. Psychologists and psycholinguists reckon that the normal speed of delivery is between five and seven syllables per second. However, it would be unwise to make that the objective standard by which we could assess fluency. If someone wanted to, he could practise saying sentences at those speeds but have a kind of staccato production – and this would not be regarded as fluent, because the smooth joining-up of elements would be missing.

What has to be joined up? Consonants and vowels; and also consonants with consonants, and to a lesser extent, vowels with vowels. Consonants combine with consonants at the beginning and end of words and syllables, and these combinations, like /br.../ and /...ld/, are called *consonant clusters*. There are many such combinations in English and they are often the source of great problems for many learners. Vowel sequences may also be a little troublesome, such as /eɪ/ and /ɒ/ in *chaotic*, for instance.

Words have to be joined up to words, and when they are, the final phoneme or phonemes of one word may affect the initial phoneme or phonemes of the following word. Phonemes get lost and added, and phonemes get changed too; these processes are called *simplifications*.

Elements of clause structure, like the subject of a clause, have to be joined up with other elements of clause structure, like verbs, or direct objects, and so on; here, the *rhythm* of an utterance is important.

Also, clauses and sentences are joined up to following clauses and sentences, and in this case, *intonation* is the significant factor.

Practice can be made in each of these areas to increase fluency of pronunciation, and we will look at each in turn in this chapter and the next.

4.1 Consonant clusters

INITIAL CLUSTERS

There are two types of initial consonant clusters, a primary set of clusters, and a secondary set that combine only with /j/ before the vowels /u, ʊ, ʊə/. The primary set is given in Table 2.

Table 2

pr	tr	kr	fr	θr	ʃr
br	dr	gr			
pl		kl	fl		sl
bl		gl			
	tw	kw		θw	sw
	dw	gw			

sp	st	sk
sm	sn	

spr	str	skr
spl		skl
		skw

The secondary set – the initial clusters with /j/ – consists of any consonant except /ð, w, r, ʃ/ and /ʒ/, followed by /j/. Some combinations are extremely infrequent: /gj-/ is represented by *gules*, *gewgaw*, /θj-/ by *thews*, /zj-/ by *Zeus*; /lj-/ is undergoing change, ie pronunciations without /j/ are becoming more and more common for *lewd*, *lure*, *lucid*, *allusions*, etc. This is true also of a number of words with /sj-/, such as *suit*, *sewer*.

FINAL CLUSTERS

Final clusters are much more numerous and may seem haphazard, but basically they are mirror images of the initial clusters. Again, it seems appropriate to divide clusters in final position into two parts: the structurally simple forms, and the derived and inflected forms – plurals, possessives, past tenses and derived forms with *-th*. First of all, consider the simple forms, as in Table 3.

Table 3

lp	lt		ltʃ	lk	lpt		lkt
lb	ld		ldʒ				
lf	lθ	ls	lʃ				
lv							
lm	ln						
mp	nt		ntʃ	ŋk	mpt	mps	ŋkt
	nd		ndʒ				
mf	nθ	ns					nst
		nz					
ps	ts, dz		ks				kst
pt			kt				
sp	st		sk				

The structurally complex clusters duplicate and extend the simple clusters. Plural and possessive morphemes yield clusters with /-s, -z/; past tense morphemes yield clusters with /-t, -d/; and derivation morphemes yield clusters with /-θ/. Historically, this last morpheme accounts for the /-lθ/ clusters too: *heal – health, weal – wealth, foul – filth*. The extension to the simple forms by these morphemes is considerable, increasing the lists of two- and three-consonant clusters, and forming the following four-consonant clusters: /-lpts/ *(he) sculpts*, /-lkts/ *(he) mulcts*, /-mpts/ *(he) prompts*, /-mpst/ *glimpsed*, /-ŋkts/ *instincts*, /-ksts/ *texts*, /-lfθs/ *twelfths*, /-ksθs/ *sixths*. However, it must be admitted that in rapid colloquial speech, each of these four-consonant clusters is regularly simplified; but in formal speech they may well be retained. Another feature to note is that as soon as a stop or fricative enters the final clusters, the following members of the cluster will share the voice-tension feature of that stop or fricative, eg /-zd, -lvz, -kst, -mpst/.

Learners will have difficulties with the consonant clusters that do not match their own pronunciation system. This is especially the case where the mother tongue has relatively few consonant clusters. These learners tend to add vowels to the beginning or end of initial and final clusters in order to spread the cluster over more than one syllable, or to add vowels in the sequence of consonants and split them into separate syllables. If C represents any consonant and V any vowel, the fullest potential syllable may have this structure: $C\ C\ C\ V\ C\ C\ C\ C$. Learners then may modify them as follows: $v\ C\ C\ C\ \ldots\ C\ C\ C\ C\ v$, or $C\ v\ C\ v\ C\ \ldots\ C\ v\ C\ v\ C\ v\ C$, etc, where v represents an inserted vowel.

In some languages, a syllable always ends in a vowel, or in a restricted number of consonants. The tendency for these learners is then to add a vowel, often /ə/, as a reflex of their mother-tongue system.

Thus, consonant clusters often need extra attention. It is not usually a problem of perception, although, admittedly, occasionally it is; if it is, then ear-training practice as described in the previous chapter has to be prescribed again. Problems concerning consonant clusters are usually simply a problem of articulation. A learner may be able to produce the elements of a cluster satisfactorily, but the combination of the elements in close sequence may prove to be problematical. Demonstration is usually sufficient, but where it is not, the teacher must resort to association and/or explanation. For instance, the initial /sp-, st-, sk-/ clusters are often preceded by a short vowel in many learners' misarticulation. If their attention is drawn to this, most can produce the clusters correctly when they are conscious of their occurrence. Imitation of /spə . . . spə/ is followed by practice of /sp-/ in isolated words, and then those words are incorporated into something worth saying. If the problem persists, then the teacher might explain as follows: 'Start off by saying /s/ and prolong it, /sss . . ./. Then add /p/ to the prolonged /s/, as /sssspə/ and say that a few times. Try to shorten the initial /s/ to /sssspə/,

/sspə/ and to /spə/.' The teacher should then substitute other vowels for /ə/ and build up actual words and phrases. The learner's problem is that by placing a vowel before /sp-/, he is producing an extra syllable. By starting off with /s/ and lengthening it, the learner's extra syllable is realised as a long 'syllabic' /s/, which can then be contracted to a short 'non-syllabic' /s/.

Other learners have difficulty with the sequence stop + /l, r, w, j/; they tend to add a vowel between the stop and the following consonant. If straightforward demonstration fails to be effective, the teacher must resort to explanation again. Stop + /l/ can be practised like this: 'Start off with /l/ and consciously keep your tongue in the /l/ position. Prolong the /l/, as /lll . . ./. Then prolong it again and close and open your lips, thus adding a series of /p/ or /b/; the series of /p/ or /b/ and the prolonged /l/ are being articulated simultaneously as $\left[\begin{smallmatrix} lllll \ldots \\ pp \end{smallmatrix}\right]$. Then, when /p/ or /b/ is articulated, hold it a little longer and allow the /l/ to emerge gradually; repeat this and try to reduce the length of the hold of /p/ or /b/, to achieve /pl-/ and /bl-/.' The same procedure is possible with initial /k/ and /g/. While /l/ is being prolonged, the learner can raise and lower the back of the tongue to form and release the velar stops. And the same procedure can be adopted with the sequence stop + /r/: 'Start off with /r/ and consciously keep your tongue in the /r/ position. Prolong it to /rrrr/ and add a series of /p/, as $\left[\begin{smallmatrix} rrrr \ldots \\ pp \end{smallmatrix}\right]$ and continue as above.'

/tr/ and /dr/ are a little more awkward, as it must be remembered that /t/ and /d/ in this context do not retain their alveolar point of articulation. Nevertheless, exactly the same procedure can be adopted, but whereas in /pr-, br-, kr-, gr-/ the /r/ element can remain fixed, in /tr-, dr-/ the tongue blade in fact moves from /r/ to make an actual (post-alveolar) total closure for the /t/ and /d/ elements. Thus the real sequence is more like $\left[\begin{smallmatrix} r \ tr \ r \ tr \ r \\ \ t \ \ \ t \end{smallmatrix}\right]$. . . . The learner need not know this, of course; but it is as well if the teacher does know what is going on. Again, exactly the same procedure can be adopted with sequences of stop + /w/ and stop + /j/, and also fricative + /l, r, w, j/. A combination of the technique of establishing /sp/ and the technique of establishing /pl/ would be necessary with persistent problems with /spl-/; and similarly, of course, with other three-consonant initial clusters.

In final consonants, similar and other problems may arise too. Again, if possible, the teacher should rely on straightforward demonstration, but he will need to resort to explanation if that does not work. One problem is the insertion of a vowel between /l/ and the following consonant(s). 'Say /l/ and prolong it, as /lll.../; gradually close the lips while the /l/ is still being produced; open the lips but keep the /l/.' (The effect is to produce something like $\left[\underset{pp°}{llllll} \ldots\right]$; the /l/ after a voiceless fortis consonant will be devoiced ḷ.) The same can be done for other consonants except those articulated with the tip and blade of the tongue: /θ, t, d, s, z, n/. In these cases, the teacher must advise the learner to consciously keep the tongue in the /l/ position until the /l/ merges into the following sound.

Final sequences of stops, such as /-pt, -kt, -bd/, are described for Received Pronunciation as a sequence of unreleased stop + released stop. If a learner consistently releases the first stop in the sequence, as [-pʰtʰ] rather than [-ptʰ], then the teacher need not be worried, as many native speakers of English do so too. If a teacher has a perfectionist on his hands, then the perfectionist must make a deliberate effort to retain the closure of the first stop while effecting the closure of the second. For instance for /-pt/, the lips must remain sealed while the tongue blade rises for the alveolar closure of /t/; for /-kt/, the back of the tongue must remain raised against the soft palate while the blade effects alveolar closure of /t/.

A more serious problem is a sequence of fricatives. It is noticeable that while a learner may have established an excellent command of the pronunciation of English, his pronunciation of *months* may let him down, because he omits the /s/ (usually) or the /θ/. Native English speakers often reduce sequences of fricatives at the ends of words or across syllable boundaries, as /fɪθs/ for *fifths* and /æsmə/ for *asthma*, but they do not reduce *months* to /mʌnθ/ or /mʌns/. This is pure articulatory gymnastics; and as in (ordinary) gymnastics a movement is taken slowly at first and then speeded up as confidence increases, so also in the case of fricative sequences. The movement of the tongue in the sequence /-θs/ has to be demonstrated; the only explanation is an obvious one: 'Hold the tongue in the /θ/ position and prolong the /θ/ and then, suddenly and sharply, draw the tongue in and upwards'. The /-θs/ has then to be reinserted into the word *months*, and other such words.

4.2 Simplifications in colloquial speech

Economy of effort is a universal trait in man and is shown clearly in his speech as it is in every aspect of his behaviour. If man can save himself some effort in his speech without causing any hindrance to the transmission of his message, then he will. Economy of effort is however constrained by various factors: for example, a driver will cut corners only to a certain extent because of the risk of accidents; if a speaker economises on articulation to such an extent that his hearers misunderstand, then he will adjust his articulation accordingly.

Simplifications are normal in colloquial speech and take a number of forms including *elision* (the loss of a sound), *assimilation* (the variation of a sound), *weak forms* and *contractions*. Simplifications are conventional and systematic and appear in different languages in different ways.

First of all, elision of consonants. The most important area is the elision of /t/ and /d/ when they occur at the end of a word after another consonant, (eg *exact*, *post*, *old*, *friend*) – if the immediately following word or morpheme begins with another consonant, the /t/ and /d/ are regularly elided in ordinary informal colloquial speech (which is, of course, what we use most of the time). Consider now the following examples: *exactly*, *postman*, *old man*, *friends*. In most varieties of English speech the previously final /t/ and /d/ are lost. This tendency to elision is so strong that if a speaker makes a determined effort to reinsert /t/ and /d/, his pronunciation sounds distinctly odd. Many examples of this can be cited: *next week*, *best man*, *West Germany*, *soft-centred*, *mashed potatoes*, *brand-new*, *hold tight*, *world record*, *kindness*, *child's*, etc. However, if the following consonant is /h/, elision does not usually take place; and if the following consonant is one of /l, w, r, j/, elision is optional. If a nasal or /l/ precedes /t/, the /t/ is retained but usually in the form of a glottal stop, eg *can't come*, *Walt Disney*. A similar instance is the loss of /k/ in similar contexts, eg *asked*.

Another common case is the loss of a fricative when two or more fricatives occur together; /θ/ is lost in *asthma*, /ð/ is lost in *clothes brush*, either /f/ or /θ/ is lost in *fifths, twelfths*. /h/ is lost in the weak forms of *have*, *has*, *had*, *he*, *his*, *him*, *her*, *who*, unless preceded by a pause; if preceded by a vowel, elision is optional. /ʃ/ is lost in the weak form of *shall*, and /w/ in the weak form of *will*.

/l/ is often lost after the vowel /ɔ/ in words like *already*, *all right*, *although*, and this phenomenon parallels exactly the historical elision of *l* in *walk*, *talk*, etc. /r/ is elided along with an unaccented vowel (usually /ə/) when another /r/ is close, eg *library* /laɪbrɪ/; *literary* /lɪtrɪ/; *temporary* /temprɪ/; *February* /febrɪ/.

Elision of vowels is mainly confined to instances in unaccented syllables and consequently implies a loss of a syllable. The loss of /ə/ after a consonant and before /r, l, n/ in an unaccented syllable immediately after an accented syllable is firmly established in

British English; as in words like *history* /hɪstrɪ/, *family* /fæmlɪ/, *reasonable* /riznəbl/ and a very large number of words ending in -ory -ery, -ary, -ury and -ily and adverbs ending in -fully, eg *carefully* /keəflɪ/. A similar form of elision is common in an initial unaccented syllable immediately before an accented syllable in informal colloquial speech, eg *correct* as /krekt/, *perhaps* as /præps/, *collect* as /klekt/, *police* as /plis/ and also *eleven* as /levn/; other such cases bring two consonants together that do not normally occur in the English sound system, eg *veranda* as /vrændə/, *syringe* as /srɪndʒ/, *pathetic* as /pθetɪk/. Another very common example is *suppose* as /spəʊz/ and often written as *s'pose*.

Another area of vowel elision is heard in RP but by no means in all British accents – the elision of the second element of a diphthong before /ə/, eg *tower* as /tɑə/. *Our* is reduced by many to /ɑ/, especially when unaccented.

Assimilation involves either a change of one phoneme for another, eg the /n/ of *ten* changes to /m/ in *ten pence*, or the addition of a phoneme, eg the /k/ that often appears between /ŋ/ and /θ/ in *length*. It is particularly important to note how /d/ and /n/ readily assimilate to the point of articulation of a following consonant. Consider the word *good* before *man, fun, thing, riddance, year, girl,* where the /d/ will switch from alveolar first to bilabial, then labio-dental, dental, post-alveolar, palato-alveolar and velar. /n/ behaves in a similar way. /t/ is slightly different in that whereas it may follow the /d/ assimilation pattern, it is more often realised as a glottal stop in these contexts: *great* in *a great man* is realised either as [greɪp] or, more commonly, as [greɪʔ]; and this applies to all the other contexts including before other alveolars: *great time* is usually rendered [greɪʔ tɑɪm], etc.

Notice too what usually happens when /t, d, s, z/ precede /j/; they become /tʃ, dʒ, ʃ, ʒ/. For example, *meet you* becomes /mitʃu/, *did you* becomes /dɪdʒu/, *this year* becomes /ðɪʃjɜ/, and *these units* becomes /ðiʒjunɪts/. (However, /t/ before /j/ is also often pronounced as a glottal stop, as above: [miʔju].) Similarly, /s, z/

often become /ʃ, ʒ/ before /ʃ/. For example, *this ship* becomes /ðɪʃ ʃɪp/ and *these ships* /ðɪʒ ʃɪps/.

One variety of addition is the appearance of /r/ after the vowels /ɑ, ɔ, ɜ, ə/ and the three centring diphthongs /ɪə, eə, ʊə/ at the ends of words when the next word begins with a vowel. For example *far* is pronounced /fɑ/ as a rule, but in *far away*, an /r/ is added: /fɑrəweɪ/. Even if there is no *r* in the spelling, /r/ is usually added: *law*, as /lɔ/, but *law and order* has the additional /r/. It is basically another case of the lack of precise articulation that is characteristic of rapid colloquial speech.

The rules of elision and assimilation vary from language to language, and the learner will unconsciously reproduce the rules of his own mother tongue as he attempts to speak informal colloquial English. The teacher will need to look out for such foreign simplifications. But the teacher must also be aware that the simplifications described here for English are typical of ordinary English colloquial speech. This is not a case of slovenly speech, but colloquial speech. And these simplifications are to be practised as such. There is absolutely no need for the teacher to insist on a /d/ in *brand-new*, for example; he might even, in fact, point out that the /d/ in *Good morning* is actually pronounced as /b/. The elisions and assimilations help fluency; to insist otherwise will hinder fluency and lead to the practice of items that native speakers themselves have abandoned in colloquial speech.

4.3 Rhythm

We defined fluency at the beginning of this chapter as the smooth joining-up of elements at an acceptable speed of delivery. Rhythm is a vital factor in the smooth joining-up of words in speech, and in particular we need to look for (1) correct word accent, (2) accent timing, (3) weak forms and (4) pauses in the right places.

Correct word accent can be practised by perceiving accented

and unaccented syllables in words and phrases through ear-training exercises, and by imitation of correct pronunciation and also by developing an awareness of the variation of accent in derived forms of words, eg 'politics, po'litical, poli'tician (where ' precedes the accented syllable). Again, it must be emphasised that these types of practice are only necessary where there is a genuine and recognisable problem. Many learners will not need anything more than straight imitation practice as was described in Chapter 2. Others will need these extra activities because of their very general difficulties with word accent and rhythm, especially those learners who have a fixed pattern of word accent and/or syllable timing in their mother tongue.

4.4 Rhythm 1: word accent

If necessary, practice in perceiving the sequence of accented and unaccented syllables in words and phrases can be in the form of ear-training exercises. Simple words of more than one syllable can be dictated, and the learners have to indicate which syllable was accented. They can do this by saying which syllable was accented (eg 'First', 'Second', 'Last', etc) or by writing the syllable number on paper (eg 1, 2, 3 or ①, ②, ③). Or else they can underline the letters of the accented syllable (eg elephant, giraffe). A kind of revision exercise might be to do this underlining of the accented syllable without the teacher dictating the word(s) at all. If a learner makes a mistake, the teacher can draw attention to the pattern of accented and unaccented syllables of a word or phrase by a kind of hum – *mMm*, or *Mmm*, etc – or other such noises, where the accented syllable is indicated by a louder and higher-pitched hum. Another way of indicating the word-accent pattern is by a series of dots, lines or crosses, where the accented syllable is shown by a larger dot, line or cross. Thus, for example, *elephant* is ●.. ; *giraffe* is .● and so on.

Getting learners to imitate is also a good way of testing whether they have perceived the accentual pattern. A teacher may get his learners to imitate a series of words where the accent falls on a different syllable. Listening to and imitating nonsense syllables is another device, for example:

'la la   la'la   la'la   'lala   la'la

Particular patterns can be practised with a group of words and phrases which each have the same pattern. For instance, the pattern ●.. can be practised with a series of words like:

quality	bachelor	luckily
quantity	yesterday	telephone
appetite	character	photograph

The learners might have to identify the pattern and then imitate the teacher's dictation or a recording, and finally have to say them themselves without any stimulus. This may then be followed up by the learners having to imitate a set of sentences that contained each of these words, and again finally having to say such sentences without any stimulus from the teacher.

Phrases and sayings might also be included amongst the words for practice. For instance, the pattern .●. could be practised with the following:

enormous	tomato	of course not
important	potato	I'm sorry
tobacco	I think so	a nightmare

Another problem in word accents is the shifting of accents from one syllable to another in derived words. The example that was given above was 'politics (first syllable accented), po'litical (second syllable accented) and poli'tician (third syllable accented). A number of rules apply to the placement of the primary accent in certain words of classical origin and these can be exploited for practice in drills. For instance, the following endings usually require the primary accent on the syllable preceding them:

-tion, -sion:	elevation, promotion, station; cohesion, occasion, persuasion
-ian:	Asian, Australian, Canadian, Christian, comedian
-ic:	atomic, comic, dramatic, economic, electric, music
-ical:	chemical, comical, economical, electrical, musical, physical
-ial, -ual:	aerial, colonial, commercial, dictatorial; continual, sensual, usual
-ious, -eous, -uous:	conscious, vicious; courteous, righteous; continuous
-ity, -ety:	captivity, electricity, finality; propriety, society
-cient:	efficient, sufficient
-itous:	circuitous
-itude:	altitude, attitude, gratitude, magnitude
-ify, -efy:	identify, qualify, terrify; stupefy; also satisfy

The ending -ise usually requires the primary accent on the syllable before the immediately preceding one:

advertise, apologise, centralise, monopolise, organise, realise, subsidise

but this tendency is not so strong now that many new words are coined with -ise, eg *hospitalise, circularise, nationalise,* with the accent on a syllable even further back.

A drill exercise could be used to practise derived forms as follows:

promote	promotion
prevent	prevention
persuade	persuasion

Instead of bare lists like these, practice sentences could be designed with the two forms:

John is hoping to be promoted. I look forward to his ...
They hope to persuade me to go. But I don't think much of their powers of ...
Professor Jones has invented yet another machine. Oh no! not another ...

Often, the only sensible means of practice is to string a series of derived words together, and imitate the teacher's stimulus or a recording. This can be followed up with practice without a stimulus, and with written practice too – underlining the accented syllable, for instance. Such a set of words might include the following:

politics, political, politician
democrat, democracy, democratic
personal, personify, personality
hypocrite, hyprocrisy, hypocritical
photograph, photographer, photographic

These words might then appear separately in practice sentences which learners have to say with and without a stimulus, for example:

What he's really interested in is politics.
Their decision was clearly political.
Yes, he would make a good politician.

Learners of a European background may often recognise the written form of a word, eg *photography*, but be completely misled by its pronunciation. The primary accent in this example is on *tog*, which might leave such a learner wondering what on earth a 'tog' is!

Word-accent contrasts present another problem area – cases like the noun 'protest (first syllable accented) and the verb pro'test (second syllable accented). Such words could be practised in pairs, but practice in sentences would make more sense, as in the following:

They protested about their treatment. Yes, we heard about their protest.
Five of them rebelled. But they caught one rebel.
They insulted his wife. It was a terrible insult.

See also Materials for pronunciation practice, page 113.

4.5 Rhythm 2: accent timing

This is not a problem that all learners have to cope with: learners with a Germanic background share the same type of rhythm as English. But learners from a French, Italian or Spanish background do have problems because of the syllable timing of their mother tongues; many African and Asian languages have syllable timing too. The problem is simply that speakers of these languages give too much prominence to the unaccented syllables of English, so that the distinction between accented and unaccented syllables is almost lost; they don't 'spring' from accent to accent as in a normal English utterance, and consequently native English speakers often have difficulty in interpreting their speech.

Tapping the rhythm or stabbing the air, as suggested at the beginning of chapter 3, might be enough for many learners, but we have to consider those who will need much fuller correction.

One form of practice is to arrange a list of utterances which have an exact pattern of accents. Learners could imitate the teacher or a recording, or they could speak simultaneously with the teacher or recording – this is called 'ghosting' or 'tracking'. The following utterances have all got the same pattern:

I think he wants to go there.   He's never very punctual.
We ought to give an answer.   She married Mary's brother.

The danger of this kind of practice is that it might easily lead to the kind of 'sing-song' reading that we associate with reciting verse. The teacher, or the recording model, must be careful to avoid this, and make the utterances sound natural.

It may be necessary to conduct this practice in such a way that the teacher beats time as he speaks. It may also be necessary to exaggerate the loudness of the accented syllables in initial practice, to impress upon the learner the importance of springing from one accent to the next. This could be done with the basic dialogues and sentence patterns of the coursebook, as in the following example (where the accented syllables are capitalised):

She's OBviously BORED.
She SEEMS to be BORED.
It LOOKS as if she's BORED.

or with the kind of supplementary material suggested above.

Utterances with regular patterns of accented and unaccented syllables can be practised in dialogues, too. Here is an example (Mortimer 1976:13):

A THIS is the FURniture.
B ISn't it TErrible!
A TErrible?
B TErrible!
A THIS is Aunt AGatha's FURniture, MARgery!
B SHE doesn't NEED it and NEIther do WE.

Mortimer's advice is that the learners should hear the dialogue a couple of times and should understand the sense of it before they start practising it. Then they should beat out the rhythm by tapping; and next, practise saying only the accented syllables as they tap, in order to consciously keep these at equal intervals. The final step is to fill in all the unaccented syllables. The recording of such dialogues is duplicated; the first rendering is accompanied by tapping – it sounds like a music teacher's metronome – and the second without it. The regularity of the beat in the recording sounds exaggerated, but is extremely effective practice.

The regularity of accents can also be practised by altering the number of unaccented syllables between the accents. An example of this is:

Which is the train for Crewe, please?
Which is the train for Manchester, please?

(The single accented syllable of *Crewe* is replaced by the accented syllable and two unaccented syllables of *Manchester*, without disturbing the regularity of accents.) The number of beats remains the same despite the increase in the number of syllables. Other examples are:

The MAN SMILED.
The MANager SMILED.

We BOUGHT a BOOK.
We have BOUGHT another BOOK.
We could have BOUGHT you another BOOK.
We ought to have BOUGHT ourselves another BOOK.

Such sets of utterances can be used for practice in the various ways already mentioned: imitation, ghosting, with and without tapping, without a stimulus, marking the primary accents by underlining, and so on.

Another technique used by some teachers is a substitution drill. An utterance is divided into separate clause elements, and each element can be replaced by another word or phrase with the same number of accents (though not necessarily the same number of syllables). Here is an example adapted from a well-known practice manual (Arnold & Tooley 1970: 29):

He	always	works alone
She	occasionally	replies in English
Joan	often	writes to Dominique

| Andrew | usually | helps my uncle |
| Christopher | never | works on the farm |

Many different utterances can be produced from this table. A learner may take the first line, or select *He occasionally works alone*, and so on. Whatever clause element he selects, he will always have the same rhythm. The teacher, of course, may do the selecting, and imitation follows.

An expansion drill is another useful technique. Either a sentence is practised by successively adding one element to another, as:

My neighbour
My neighbour is for ever
My neighbour is for ever complaining to me
My neighbour is for ever complaining to me about something.

Or, alternatively, a simple sentence is added to and expanded, as:

My neighbour complains.
My neighbour is complaining.
My neighbour is for ever complaining.
My neighbour is for ever complaining to me.
My neighbour is for ever complaining to me about something.

Some teachers prefer to conduct the first type backwards – 'back-chaining'. It has the advantage of preserving the original intonation of the basic sentence, as well as providing practice in rhythm, as:

about something
complaining to me about something
for ever complaining to me about something
My neighbour is for ever complaining to me about something.

See also Materials for pronunciation practice, page 113.

4.6 Rhythm 3: weak forms

This 'pacing' of speech, which we have just been discussing, this springing from one accent to the next regardless of the number of intervening unaccented syllables, leads us to consider the matter of weak forms. One of the effects of accent timing in English is the weakening of the form of many 'grammatical' words, such as pronouns, conjunctions and prepositions. Fluency will be improved by practising the weak forms of these words in phrases and sentences. Note that a weak form ought not to be practised in isolation, because there is a strong tendency to produce the 'full' form of such a word when you cite it.

Weak forms can be practised in short phrases at first. We can take as an example the sequence of *for* and *a(n)* in the following phrases:

for a second	for a penny	for a boy
for a minute	for a pound	for a girl
for an hour		
for a day		
for a week		

These can then be practised in longer utterances:

He had it for a second.
He had it for a minute.

Two for a penny.
Ten for a pound.

Here's one for a boy.
Here's one for a girl.

The same range of techniques is available; imitation, ghosting, with and without tapping, without a stimulus, and so on. The weak forms of grammatical items can be practised in this way, and all the contracted forms, too; eg *What's* for *What is*:

What is the time? /wɒts/
What is the date?

See also Materials for pronunciation practice, page 113.

4.7 Rhythm 4: pauses

Less consideration has been given to pausing in practice materials in English pronunciation, probably because it seems to fall between two stools, rhythm and intonation. Pausing is rhythmical but also marks the boundaries of intonation units, and a great deal of published practice material concentrates on single utterances which have a given rhythmical pattern and consist of a single intonation pattern. One of the most important uses of pauses in English is the syntactic function, and we shall concentrate on that one. (I am assuming that beginners will not be taught the contrasting function of pause; they will simply imitate the teacher's pronunciation of an utterance, unaware of a potential means of syntactical contrast.)

Pauses have to be noticed, and so some training in perception may be necessary. A pair of sentences like the following can be used to help a learner take note of the pause:

My brother who is abroad ...   (Which brother? The one who is abroad)

My brother ʌ who is abroad ...   (Only one brother; he happens to be abroad)

The difference in meaning can be given, and more examples can follow:

The book that I'm now writing   (Which book? The one which ...)

The book ∧ that I'm now
writing

(Only one book, which I
happen ...)

John my son ∧ and his wife ...   (John is my son)
John ∧ my son ∧ and his wife   (John is not my son)
...

Once the difference of meaning has been grasped, then the learner can be asked a kind of comprehension question: 'Is only one brother or more than one brother implied?', etc.

My brother who is abroad ...   (More than one brother)
My brother ∧ who is abroad ...   (Only one brother)
The book ∧ that I am now   (Only one book)
writing ...
John ∧ my son ∧ and his wife   (John is not my son)

After the training in perceiving the pauses and the test of comprehension, imitation exercises should follow, with beats being tapped out; a beat will also be needed for the pause, as:

My BROther – who is aBROAD ...

This is not an easy exercise, and it is expected that only more advanced learners who can appreciate the difference in meaning will practise this kind of pause exercise.

5 Intonation

Intonation requires separate treatment in the discussion of pronunciation because many teachers are unaware of its forms and functions and, consequently, are unaware of its importance. This chapter is an attempt to convince sceptical teachers of the value of teaching intonation. Many feel that intonation is unteachable because of its complexity or intangibility: and certainly many guides to pronunciation offer considerably less help on intonation than on consonants, vowels, diphthongs and the word accents. First of all, we have an introduction to the structure of intonation; secondly, an introduction to its functions; thirdly, a guide to detecting errors; and fourthly, a guide to teaching it.

5.1 Structure of intonation

Intonation can be defined as the linguistic use of pitch in utterances; we are not concerned in the study of intonation with any aesthetic or artistic use of pitch, nor with tone languages like Chinese, which make use of pitch variations in words, as well as in utterances.

Intonation is systematic, like all the other elements in pronunciation that we have discussed so far. Admittedly, intonation is personal, but it is also conventional. Many have the idea that intonation is so subjective and individual a matter that it defies generalisation; but that is not true. Many also feel that the only thing a person can do in the study of intonation is to present vague and general impressions; but that is not true either. The very fact that people take note of the way something is said ('It's not what he said, but the way he said it . . .') and interpret it to mean something shows that there is some agreement or understanding between speakers of a language in the realm of intonation. Intonation is systematic, and the system can be described.

Intonation is structured. It has units and parts of units, in the same way that rhythm has units (ie the syllables). Consider the utterance:

What on earth did you want to do that for?

said without any break or interruption. Most native speakers of English would probably highlight the word *that*, and would do so by making that syllable louder and higher in pitch than the other syllables; they would also probably pronounce the final word *for* in a low pitch. People may differ in the way they move from the high pitch of *that* to the low pitch of *for*: some would allow the pitch of the voice to fall during the *that* syllable from high to low, while others would keep the pitch of *that* high and allow the pitch of the voice to drop or jump down in the transition from *that* to *for*:

that   for   or   that   for

(Say it yourself and see which way you do it.)

The whole utterance is termed an 'intonation unit' (or 'tone unit', or 'tone group'); the *that* syllable, which is most prominent and carries the significant level or movement of pitch, is termed the 'tonic' syllable (or nucleus); the tonic syllable divides the intonation unit into the pre-tonic segment and the tonic segment (which includes the tonic syllable and any post-tonic syllables, called the 'tail'). The intonation structure of this utterance can be illustrated in this way:

What on earth did you want to do	that for?
pre-tonic segment	*tonic segment*

This particular utterance begins with an accented syllable.

The following one can be pronounced with four unaccented syllables before the first accented one:

It would have been better not to have paid for it

We will assume that *paid* is the tonic, and so all the syllables before it are called the pre-tonic segment. The first syllable of *better* is the first accented syllable of the pre-tonic, and it is an important one because the pitch of the whole utterance is described by reference to the pitch of that syllable. The pre-tonic is divided then into two sub-sections, (1) the 'head' (from the first accented syllable, *bet-*, up to the tonic) and (2) the 'pre-head' (the unaccented syllables before the beginning of the head). The intonation of this utterance is then illustrated as follows:

It would have been	better not to have	paid for it
pre-head	*head*	*tonic tail*
pre-tonic segment		*tonic segment*

The tonic must be present in an intonation unit; it carries the extra prominence and the important level or change in pitch which is the essential factor in intonation. (In our examples, the tonic will always be underlined.) The other elements may happen not to be present in any given unit; for instance in:

What on earth did you want to do that for?

there is no pre-head. In:

It might have been

might would be tonic and *it* a pre-head without a head since there is no accented syllable in the pre-tonic. In:

Listen to him

the intonation unit actually begins with the tonic (*Li-*) and there are no pre-tonic syllables at all. Furthermore, in:

It's fifty-six pence

there is no tail following the tonic *pence*. And in a single-syllable utterance, like 'Right!', 'Yes', 'No', 'Well', 'Oh', 'Fine!', the intonation unit consists only of a tonic and nothing more. Thus the tonic is obligatory, and the pre-head, head and tail are optional (or 'circumstantial').

Intonation units do not usually come in isolation. In the above examples we have treated them as such, simply to discuss the structure of the unit. But intonation units usually come in sequence and we need to know how to identify the boundary between one unit and the one following, and so on. Generally speaking, the number of tonics perceived in a stretch of speech gives the (same) number of intonation units in that stretch. The boundary may be identified by a slight pause, which may however be long enough for the speaker to gain his breath, or it may be identified by a change of pitch, which indicates that the pitch of a tail has come to an end: this is particularly noticeable in unaccented syllables. The division of a stretch of speech into discrete intonation units is referred to as 'tonality'. (Once a group of people have been given a little training in tonality analysis, the correlation amongst them in analysing the tonality of a recorded piece of conversation is surprisingly good).

Tonality is one of the three sub-systems at work interdependently in intonation. A second sub-system is referred to as 'tonicity', which is concerned with the placement of the tonic syllable in any given intonation unit. In most of the examples given so far in this section, the tonic has been on the accented syllable of the final lexical item in the intonation unit – not necessarily the final word, which may be a grammatical word like *for*, *it*, *been*, *him*. There is such a strong tendency in English for the tonic to fall on the final lexical item that we can regard this as the normal placement. The normal placement of the tonic is known as 'neutral tonicity'. Those cases where the tonic falls elsewhere are referred to as cases of 'marked tonicity'; the tonic may either fall on a lexical item that is not final in the intonation unit, or it may fall on a grammatical item. These two cases of marked tonicity can be illustrated as follows:

It costs fifty-<u>six</u> pence
Listen to <u>him</u>

where the first might suggest a contradiction to a previous statement of cost and the second a contrast.

The third sub-system in intonation is 'tone', which is the set of distinctive pitch movements which accompany the tonic. There are five basic distinctive pitch movements, or 'tones' (or 'tunes') in English, which can all be illustrated with the expression *OK*:

tone 1 falling		(= 'I'm OK', eg in response to the question 'How are you?')
tone 2 rising high		(= 'Are you OK?')
tone 3 rising low		(= 'I agree')
tone 4 falling-rising		(= 'I agree, but . . .', expressing doubt or reservation)
tone 5 rising-falling		(= 'I didn't expect that')

There is more to the tone system than this, as each tone has its variations, and each tone has a particular set of pitch variations in the pre-tonic segment, but it is not possible to go into further details here.

To recap on the sub-systems of intonation: a stretch of speech is likely to consist of a number of discrete intonation units (tonality), each of which must somewhere in its structure contain a tonic (tonicity) which itself bears a distinctive movement of pitch (tone). The notation that we adopt is as follows: ‖ denotes an intonation unit boundary; <u>underlining</u> denotes the tonic syllable; and the numbers 1 to 5 denote the particular tone as given above. For example:

‖1   It costs fifty-six <u>pence</u> ‖

5.2   Functions of intonation

Intonation performs a number of different roles in English. Perhaps the most important function – though possibly the least obvious – is to convey pieces of information as the speaker conceives them. Think of a person's contribution to a conversation; he may have to work up to the main point he wishes to make, and different pieces of information will have to be related together in one way or another, and he does this by presenting one 'block' of information first, and then building on it, qualifying it or repeating it, etc, with a further block. Here is the transcript of what a lady said in a conversation, after she had been forced to leave her house because of an invasion of rats:

‖ I'm too <u>scared</u> to go back ‖ I wouldn't live in <u>there</u> at the moment ‖ for <u>anything</u> ‖ It's a <u>nightmare</u> ‖ There must be <u>hundreds</u> of them ‖ I won't go <u>back</u> ‖ until the place is <u>clear</u> ‖ I shall <u>stay</u> with <u>friends</u>‖

Each intonation unit is, in fact, a unit, or block of information; the intonation units give expression to the structure of information as the lady conceived it – she knew what she wanted to say and she broke up the whole into manageable pieces, that is, pieces not only manageable to her, but to her hearers as well. Thus, information structure is communicated in the tonality system.

The role of intonation in information is seen in the tonicity system too. The tonic expresses the focus of information. Consider the following paradigm of tonic shifting:

‖ <u>All</u> the girls swim well ‖
‖ All the <u>girls</u> swim well ‖
‖ All the girls <u>swim</u> well ‖
‖ All the girls swim <u>well</u> ‖

The last item represents the normal placement of the tonic (neutral tonicity); the others represent marked tonicity and each indicates a new focus of information, such that, for instance, in the first item probably a contrast is being made with a previous statement or a previously held opinion that only some girls could swim well; similarly for the second and third items.

In the first intonation unit of the lady's utterance above, *scared* is the focus of information. Note that there is no contradiction between what is stated here about the focus of information and what was previously stated (page 88) on the usual placement of the tonic; it so happens that English speakers usually present new information at the end of an intonation unit, but this is not always the case. The focus of information, or new information, is expressed as the tonic; what is expressed in the rest of the structure of the unit is classed as 'given' information. The speaker, at least, treats it as given, believing or assuming (or even insinuating) that the hearer is, or should be, already aware of it. So, for instance, the lady in the above conversation, knows that her hearers are aware of her circumstances and she assumes that they will agree that there is no question of going back – so there is no need to highlight that part of the unit. In the following unit in that conversation, she knows that her hearers are well aware that the rats are there now – so there is no need to focus their attention on *at the moment*.

If somebody asserts:

‖ <u>All</u> the girls swim well ‖

he is assuming that his hearers already know about the girls and they have been talking or thinking about their standard of swimming. Focus of information is expressed through the tonicity system and by implication given information is also expressed by this system, which includes the speaker's treatment of information as already known by the hearer, as having been already introduced into the conversation, or as being self-evident from the physical setting or from the logical development of the conversation.

A second function of English intonation is the expression of discourse or speech functions. It is principally the tone system that performs this role; for instance, statements without any emotional or attitudinal colouring have tone 1, the falling tone; 'yes/no' (or polar) questions, again without any emotional or attitudinal colouring have tone 2, the rising high tone; *wh-* (or non-polar) questions have tone 1; and commands have tone 1. Although statements are usually expressed in declarative clauses they can be expressed in (grammatically) interrogative clauses too:

‖1 Isn't he like his <u>father</u> ‖

That is clearly not a question, but a statement. Similarly:

‖1 Do that <u>again</u> ‖1 and you're <u>fired</u> ‖

is a statement (of warning) not a command. And a verbless utterance like:

‖1 The bigger, the <u>better</u> ‖

is also a statement. The unifying factor in these statements, which are non-declarative clauses, is the falling tone; intonation overrides the grammar and expresses the discourse function. It could also be easily demonstrated that questions do not entirely depend on an interrogative clause type; nor do commands on imperative clauses. In fact, it has been maintained that it is a feature of British speech that most commands are not couched in imperative clauses. For example:

‖1 You <u>must</u> be back by six ‖

Some utterances with identical words can be differentiated by tone alone in order to express discourse functions. An obvious example is a clause with a tag:

‖ You're <u>coming</u>, ‖ <u>aren't</u> you ‖

The tag *aren't you* can be spoken with either a falling or a rising tone; if it is spoken with a falling tone, it expresses a statement; but with a rising tone, a question. The difference between the statement tag and the question tag is purely a matter of intonation.

The third function of English intonation is closely related to the second one. It is the expression of attitudes and emotions. For instance, when we are surprised, the falling of tone 1 starts from a higher pitch than normal. Compare the pitch differences in the following statement, first spoken normally and then with surprise:

‖ They are on their way <u>now</u> ‖

The pitch difference on the tonic syllable *now* can be shown like this:

On the other hand, when we comment about something that usually takes place and are expressing expectation rather than surprise, the falling tone of tone 1 starts from a lower pitch than normal. The difference can be shown like this:

‖ `He's probably for<u>got</u>ten ‖

<table>
<tr><td>\̲ ̲ ̲.̲ (normal)</td><td>╲̲ ̲.̲ (expected)</td></tr>
<tr><td>(for-)<u>gotten</u></td><td>(for-)<u>gotten</u></td></tr>
</table>

The high fall is referred to as tone 1 +, the low fall as tone 1 −.

Agreement to a request is indicated by a slight rise, as in tone 3:

‾‾‾‾╱‾

(Can you help me for a moment?) ‖ All <u>right</u> ‖

Reservation or doubt is indicated by the fall-rise, as in tone 4. If we take the following example, it could be expressed as a straightforward statement with tone 1, but the element of reservation is added if tone 4 is used instead:

‾‾‾‾‾‾╲   (reservation)

‖ It's a bit <u>long</u> ‖

‾‾‾‾‾‾‿‾‾   (statement)

A strong assertion can be indicated by the rise-fall, as in tone 5, in addition to tone 1 +; thus:

‾‾‾⌒‾‾‾

‖ It's <u>nice</u>, Charlotte ‖   (strong assertion)

Much more could have been said about English intonation than has been possible to include in this brief introduction; indeed, a separate publication is needed in order to explain the full range of intonation forms and intonation functions. What has been attempted here is to give a brief outline of some of the main points: intonation is an important part of pronunciation; it is systematic and structured; it accompanies every utterance and is an integral part of the communication system of English.

5.3 Detecting errors in intonation

If a learner has given a response that is accurate as far as the consonants, vowels and word accent are concerned, but is faulty in some way in intonation, then reference to what has just been outlined should help in the diagnosis. Perhaps the tonality of the utterance was at fault. Did the learner, for instance, utter the response as two intonation units instead of as one, or as one instead of as two? An example:

‖ He's coming ‖ is he ‖   as opposed to   ‖ He's coming is he ‖

In the first case there are two separate identifiable intonation units; normally, the first unit would have tone 1 (falling) and the second tone 2 (rising high), thus:

‖ 1 He's coming ‖ 2 is he ‖   as opposed to   ‖ 1 He's coming is he ‖

In the second of the two examples, there is only one intonation unit with a tonic only on *com-*; as a statement, tone 1 would be expected. There is a difference in meaning in this pair. The first utterance (with two intonation units) is a statement with a *question* tag; the second (with only one intonation unit) is more of a comment on information just received and often includes a hint of criticism. There is, then, a clear change of meaning. A learner may not realise this: he may intend one version but happen to actually say the other.

Another example of a clash of tonality is more common. Compare the two possible versions of this sentence:

He has a cup of tea normally.

If there is a tonality break before *normally*, then we would interpret the utterance as a statement (*He has a cup of tea*) followed by a comment (*normally*). If there is no tonality break, the speaker would appear to suggest that the person has a cup of tea in a normal way, in contrast, possibly, to someone else who has a cup of tea in an abnormal way! This is apparently a common mistake by learners from a particular background; they may intend the first version but happen to say the second and cause raising of eyebrows! It should not be too difficult to think of similar examples which could lead to great hilarity. The point is, whether the consequence is hilarious or baffling, wrong tonality is an error.

Problems with tonicity may be even more common. In English, we can place the tonic almost anywhere in an intonation unit, although we do generally have a preference for placing it on the last lexical item (see page 88). In other languages, the placing of the tonic is more fixed than in English; and learners of English with such linguistic backgrounds may well find it very difficult to accommodate to the more flexible placing of the tonic.

Problems with tone are probably the commonest: the learner's voice going up instead of down, and down instead of up. Some have difficulty in producing the fall-rise of tone 4 and the rise-fall of tone 5, simply because their mother tongues do not have those tones in their intonation system.

Thus, if the teacher detects a fault in intonation, the following can be usefully checked: firstly, the *tonality* (Has the learner got the right number of intonation units in his response?); secondly, the *tonicity* (Has the learner placed the tonic on the right syllable?); and thirdly, the *tone* (Has the learner used the right tone on the tonic syllable?). In addition to those questions, the learner may have mistaken the meaning of the intonation form that he has used – he may have used an intonation form for the wrong function, or he may have got the pitch pattern of the pretonic segment or the tail wrong. There is much, then, that can go wrong in intonation.

5.4 Teaching intonation

If so much can go wrong, a teacher may well feel that the task is too great. But he must consider at least three points: firstly, intonation is too important a part of spoken communication to be ignored or neglected; secondly, intonation is systematic and can be handled systematically; and thirdly, and strangely, a native speaker of English is more likely to tolerate mistakes in consonants, vowels and word accent than in intonation. This may be thought strange and, in some sense, unfair; but it is common observation that native English speakers tolerate, and even expect, mistakes in the learners' pronunciation of words. This is because native speakers are aware, in a general way, of the problems associated with consonants, vowels and diphthongs, and also with word accent. They may also realise the difficulty of the apparent lack of consistency between spelling and pronunciation and consequently express some sympathy with the learner. But they may not be at all so conscious of the crucial role of intonation in their own speech – either because they have never had to think about it, or because there is nothing that consistently represents the effect of intonation in the written form of the language.

For example, if a learner intends to make a straightforward statement, he might do so using the intonation form that corresponds to straightforward statements in his mother tongue: but what if that particular intonation form actually corresponds to, say, an 'aggressive' or 'complaining' intonation in English? He will be interpreted by most English speakers as aggressive or as a continual moaner – which would be most unfortunate for both parties. The learner does not intend to be rude or a moaner, but the native English speaker does not realise that what has happened is simply a linguistic error of the same type as the mispronunciation of a word. The teacher can help a great deal and is therefore encouraged to persevere in the teaching of intonation.

There are three principles that a teacher should bear in mind with respect to intonation. Firstly, he should try to *establish accurate imitation of intonation right from the beginning* – accuracy in all the elements of pronunciation, including rhythm and intonation. Get the learner to imitate your intonation, or the intonation of a native English speaker recorded on tape. Check quickly, mentally, on tonality (Did he divide the response correctly into separate intonation units, if more than one was used?); tonicity (Did he get the tonic syllable in the right place?); and tone (Did he get the right pitch movement on the tonic syllable?). A teacher will not be able to do this quick mental checking for each response from each learner, but he should do so if the intonation of a response sounds different from that of the stimulus.

A second principle is that a teacher should *use the more normal intonation forms in initial practice* (see pages 84ff) and leave the refinements till later. The intonation of the opening dialogue in Coles & Lord 1974:7, for instance, should be the most frequently used forms in greetings: the dialogue should not be overacted with less usual intonation forms. The intonation of the dialogue might go as follows:

Arthur	Good morning, Mr Steele. (Or, possibly: Good morning, Mr Steele.)
Mr Steele	Ah, you're here, Arthur.
Arthur	Yes, I am .... Good morning, Mary.
Mary	Good morning, Arthur. How are you?
Arthur	Very well, thank you. And you?
Mary	Fine, thanks.

This scene could be made very much more dramatic, but it would be a mistake to practise it in a very dramatic way. Your learners will want to greet people most of the time in a simple, ordinary way, not melodramatically; otherwise, they will drive people to distraction each time they are greeted!

The third principle is that a teacher should *introduce a new intonation form carefully and deliberately*, and not accidentally or randomly. Admittedly, it is occasionally impossible not to use a new intonation form accidentally, as a result of unexpected or unplanned circumstances or reactions, but this should be the exception rather than the rule, and should not lead to impromptu practice. In other words, the teaching of intonation should be as planned as every other part of language teaching. Try to introduce new intonation forms only when you begin a new chapter or dialogue. We can take an example from Unit 2 of Ttofi 1978. It is an intermediate course and so learners should be aware of the more basic intonation forms. In dialogue C of Unit 2, the sentence:

What! I can't be served if I'm not over eighteen?

is one of a number of sentences to be practised. The intonation to accompany that sentence will probably be a new one, and that sentence and others like it should be practised explicitly with that intonation. The tone on *What!* is tone 2 (rising high); the pitch of the pre-tonic segment of the next intonation unit is kept on a high level, and the voice jumps down between *eight-* and *-teen* in order to rise steeply for the tone 2 on *-teen*, thus:

‖2 <u>What</u>! ‖2 I can't be served if I'm not over eigh<u>teen</u>? ‖

Other similar utterances would occur in the dialogue exercise:

What! I can't be served if I don't leave my children outside in the garden?
What! I can't be served in this bar if I'm not eating too?
What! You don't cash cheques if we're not regular customers?

Each of these utterances should be practised with the same intonation pattern. They may be practised in isolation at first with particular attention devoted to intonation, and then learners can perform the dialogue in pairs as a role-play. This intonation pattern, tone 2 on *What!* and the high-pitched pre-tonic before a second tone 2, has then to be introduced and practised with a particular type of dialogue in an obvious situation, expressing amazement in question form.

If an individual or a group of learners consistently gets a particular intonation form wrong, then it might be as well if the teacher points out the mistake directly. He can do this by contrasting the wrong form with the form required, or by highlighting or even exaggerating the point of difficulty. 'No, not *xxxx*, but *yyyy*. Listen *yyyy*, and again . . .'. Or, 'Listen, *yyYy, yyYy*, not *xXxx*'. If the wrong form suggests a different meaning in English, then that difference of meaning can be pointed out to the learners. This will add some point to the matter. 'If you say that, it means "a" in English, not "b" .'

Very few contrastive studies have been published in the area of intonation, but where one is available, and it is relevant, it could be well used to predict the kind of mistakes that a given group of learners are likely to make. To be forewarned is to be forearmed. So, for example, if the mother tongue has a high rising tone for the tonic syllable of a *wh-* question, (as is the case in Dutch, for example) it should not be surprising to hear speakers of that language reproducing the high rising tone for an English *wh-*question. But the usual tone for an English *wh-*question is tone 1, the falling tone.

A contrastive study of intonation in the mother tongue and English will often reveal that learners have difficulty in reproducing the complex pitch movement of tones 4 and 5. Another difficulty may be in perceiving the difference between the rising high tone 2 and the rising low tone 3. The pitch pattern of pre-tonic segments may also be a source of difficulty, especially as different attitudes may be expressed by them; for instance, the 'bouncy' and 'listing' pre-tonics before tone 1, and the low-pitched level pre-tonics before tones 2 and 3.

A kind of ear-training exercise can be used with intonation, as with consonants, vowels and diphthongs. A pair of utterances can be given with identical words and rhythm, and the learner has to listen for any change of intonation. He may merely have to respond 'Same' or 'Different'. The utterances may be single words like *Yes, No, Well, Right, OK* or phrases or whole sentences. Tones can obviously be tested in this way:

Right   Right   (same)

Right   Right   (different)

You've paid, haven't you?

You've paid, haven't you?   (different)

You've bought one, haven't you?

You've bought one, haven't you?   (same)

Tonicity, too, can be tested in this way:

They've all come
They've all come   (different)

They're all here
They're all here   (same)

Tonality can also be tested in this way:

‖ He's coming ‖ is he? ‖
‖ He's coming ‖ is he? ‖   (same)

‖ He's here ‖ is he? ‖
‖ He's here is he? ‖   (different)

The next step after this simple type of exercise, where a learner only has to match one utterance with another, is to actually identify a difference. In the above example with differences, a learner would have to distinguish the high rise and the low rise in the first case:

Right   (high rise)   Right   (low rise)

the rise and the fall in the second case:

... <u>haven't</u> you   (high rise)
... <u>haven't</u> you?   (fall)

the difference in tonicity in the third case (*come – all*) and the difference in tonality in the fourth case.

Another example with a pre-tonic pitch variation:

·	·	·	·	╱	·
Are	you	going	to	<u>tell</u>	me?

·	·	·	·	╱	·
Are	you	going	to	<u>tell</u>	me?

This could be a same/different exercise or an identification exercise ('Was the pitch of the pre-tonic low and level?' 'Yes/No'). Or it could be a kind of interpretation exercise. This third type is rarely conducted but it would be extremely useful, and very effective in establishing an intonation form with its meaning. In this example, the low, level pitch pattern of the pre-tonic indicates a concern or sympathetic interest on the part of the speaker, whereas the steadily falling pre-tonic pattern indicates a neutral seeking after information.

Are you going to <u>tell</u> me?
Is there anything <u>I</u> can <u>do</u> for you?
Can I <u>help</u>?
Can I <u>go</u> and <u>get</u> it for you?

Such questions can all be practised with a low, level pitch pattern in the pre-tonic at first in order to establish the association form with its meaning. Afterwards, this intonation form can be interspersed with the neutral form, and learners can be asked to interpret the forms they hear. The neutral form should be familiar to the learners long before the form showing concern is taught; this latter form is best introduced in connection with a dialogue or situation where this kind of concern is appropriate.

This interpretation type of exercise can be used in all parts of the intonation system to introduce, practise and test the various functions and meanings conveyed by intonation in English. Some further examples:

You've <u>paid</u>, <u>haven't</u> you?   (statement or question?)
You've <u>bought</u> one, <u>haven't</u> you?   (statement or question?)

It's a bit <u>long</u>   (expressing definiteness or reservation?)
It's rather ex<u>pen</u>sive   (expressing definiteness or reservation?)

Oh no I <u>won't</u>   (expressing definiteness or contradiction?)
Oh no I <u>won't</u>   (expressing definiteness or contradiction?)

Where there is a list of examples being used for drill practice, the tendency to intone them as a list must be resisted. The 'listing' form has a slight rise at the end of each item except the last one (see page 99), and it would be very easy to fall into the temptation of substituting this form for whichever intonation form was supposed to be being practised.

Some intonation drills are constructed in such a way that the learner has to change the form of intonation that he has heard in the stimulus to another one. For instance, if the stimulus has a tag with a rising tone, the learner has to reproduce the same words and rhythm, but with a falling tone on the tonic syllable. This is really quite difficult; it is also an exercise in practising only the intonation form without getting the learner to concentrate on function or meaning – and there are easier and more effective ways of doing that.

Another excellent way of helping a learner establish the association of intonation form with function is discussion. The teacher might get his class of learners to think how they would intone a particular utterance in order to create a given effect in English. This could be either a single sentence to be said in many different ways or a whole dialogue. For instance, a group might discuss different ways to intone:

He seems to have fallen asleep

either to merely give information, or to express surprise, anger or expectation, etc. A whole dialogue could be studied; for example:

Young customer	A pint of shandy, please.
Pub landlord	I'm sorry, sir, but I can't serve you if you're not over eighteen.
Young customer	What! I can't be served if I'm not over eighteen?
Pub landlord	I'm sorry, sir, but under no circumstances can you be served if you're not over eighteen.

(These examples are from Ttofi 1978: Units 1 and 2.) This type of activity can only be expected after learners have been introduced to a range of intonation forms and thus it can be thought of only as an advanced exercise. But, in fact, a similar type of exercise can be conducted at a lower level: 'How would you say that to make it sound like a request, (or a query, a command, etc)?'. For example:

Shut the door (a request = 'If you wouldn't mind')
                 (a query   = 'Is that what you really want me to do?')
                 (a command = 'Do it!')

Another example of discussion activity is to interpret a speaker's attitude from a tape-recording by asking such questions as 'Why did the speaker say it like that?' or 'What feelings did the speaker express?'. This particular type of question can relate not just to tone and pre-tonic pitch, but to tonicity and tonality as well. Questions about tonicity might require such answers as 'Because he is contrasting x with y', or, 'Because he has referred to *x* before and so he stresses *y* now', or, 'Because *x* can be seen by the person he's speaking to, and so the speaker does not have to draw attention to it'. The answers to tonality questions would have to relate mainly to the way in which the speaker structured the message he was giving. Questions on tonicity and tonality would be really only effective with intermediate and advanced students, but elementary matters in tonicity could be introduced at a fairly early stage.

A few examples of tonicity practice are included in Dickinson & Mackin 1969. After a note on the functions of the tonic syllable and a couple of examples, the learner is expected to listen to an utterance, interpret it and continue it by selecting the appropriate continuation from a list of possibilities (pages 33ff). For instance, given the clause:

I can't see very well with my glasses now . . .

the continuation depends on where the tonic syllable (referred to in the book as 'the main stress in the sentence') lies. If it lies on *now*, then the learner is expected to choose *but I could when I bought them* from the list offered. The list of possibilities also includes the following:

but John can
but I can see well with yours
but I can see quite well
but John can see well with his
but I can see well if I don't wear them

The original clause is uttered with the tonic shifted from one word to another; so that for the first of the above continuations, the learner would have to listen out for the utterance with the tonic on the first word, *I*; for the second, the tonic must be on *my*, and so on. (Perhaps you would like to work out the other possibilities for yourself!) In this exercise, then, the original clause is intoned in different ways for different continuations. Instead of a continuation, the exercise might require an appropriate choice from a number of possible responses, for example:

but you could when you bought them, couldn't you?
but John can, can't he?
but you can see well with mine, can't you?

Alternatively, the shifting of the tonic might be practised in responses to other comments. For instance, if we take the following response:

Oh/No, I thought he was here.

it may be a response to the comments:

1 He's gone away.
2 He isn't here.
3 *She* is here.
4 You said you were *sure* he was here.
5 They said they thought he was here.

The learner has to listen to the comments 1–5 and give the response with the appropriate tonicity. In reply to 1, he is expected to say:

Oh, I thought he was <u>here</u>

In reply to 4, he is expected to say:

No, I <u>thought</u> he was here
etc.

Another type of tonicity exercise is to take a dialogue and study it in order to decide where the tonic syllables in each intonation unit would appropriately fall. Here is a simple example from Hill (1965: 1ff):

'Good morning, Michael. When did you get back from your holiday?'

'Yesterday evening. We expected to get home just after lunch, but the train was very late because of the floods.'

'Oh, yes, I read about those. Did you see them?'

'We certainly did. In fact, for several hours, we wished our train was a boat.'

'Was it as bad as that?'

'Yes, when the river started to rise ...'

The learner is expected to underline the syllable (or, at least, the word) where the tonic is likely to fall. For instance, on <u>morn</u>-, <u>hol</u>-, <u>eve</u>-. (Try to identify the remaining tonic syllables for yourself!)

Tonality exercises are more difficult to devise; they reflect the different ways in which a stretch of speech may be divided up into intonation units. Examples of the change in meaning through a change in tonality have already been given earlier in this chapter (page 94). The grammatical function of pause is also really a matter of tonality:

My brother ∧ who is abroad ∧ is getting married
My brother who is abroad ∧ is getting married

The pause after *brother* in the first example is, in fact, a tonality boundary. Another similar example is:

Old men and women

Does *old* refer just to *men* or to *women* as well? It depends if there is a pause after *men* or not. Compare:

Old men ∧ and women
Old men and women

In the first example, the pause indicates that *old* refers to *men* only; the lack of pause in the second indicates that *old* refers to both *men* and *women*.

One more example of tonality contrast will be given. Consider the sentence:

He didn't come because of the money.

It can have two meanings depending on tonality. If a pause (marking a tonality boundary) occurs after *come*, the following phrase indicates the reason why he did not come: the matter of money deterred him from coming. But if there is no pause there, and that sentence is uttered as one single intonation unit, then a different meaning is conveyed: it was *not* because of the money that he decided to come; it was for some other reason that he came. (Have you grasped the second sense? If not, say the sentence again as one intonation unit, with the tonic on *money* and with a fall-rise tone.)

Pairs of sentences illustrating all these changes of meaning through tonality can be given as identification and interpretation exercises. For example:

Old men and women   (Who is old? Are the women old?)
Old men ∧ and women   (Who is old? Are the women old?)

Old books ∧ and newspapers   (What is old? Are the newspapers old?)
Old boots and shoes   (What is old? Are the shoes old?)

Another example:

He's here ∧ is he?   (a query or a critical comment?)
He's here is he   (a query or a critical comment?)

She's gone has she   (a query or a critical comment?)
They've come ∧ have they?   (a query or a critical comment?)

(In these examples the learners will, of course, be listening, not reading transcriptions like the above.)

Intonation is a vast topic but this section will nevertheless have given you some ideas of how intonation can be tackled in the classroom.

See also Materials for pronunciation practice, page 113.

Conclusion

We have now examined in some detail all the elements of pronunciation (except paralinguistic features, see page 5) and ways in which to teach them. The primary consideration has been the pronunciation of English, but the programme and techniques presented here can easily be applied to teaching the pronunciation of any language.

Pronunciation teaching needs to be *integrated* as much as possible with the rest of what makes up language teaching – grammar, vocabulary and so on. But there are times when pronunciation problems have to be *isolated* for particular attention and practice. Such practice is not an end in itself, but a means to producing *accurate* and *fluent* pronunciation, which, together with a control of grammar, vocabulary, style, function and discourse, constitutes effective communication.

The basic strategy is *imitation* of utterances (sentences, phrases, etc), supplemented by practice in specific problem areas. Such practice – most of it can be called drilling – is fundamental, because most pronunciation problems involve training the organs of speech (and the ears) to do things that they are not used to doing. This drilling may be conducted first individually and then chorally; if the drilling is done chorally first, it is difficult to know whether all the individuals are imitating accurately. If, by initial individual drilling, the teacher can establish that all the learners (or, at least, most of them) can perform accurately and fluently, then he can be reasonably satisfied that they are imitating accurately and fluently in a choral response.

Accuracy is not to be elevated above fluency. Both are required; if anything, fluency should receive more emphasis. Consonants, vowels and diphthongs are not the only elements in pronunciation that need to be taught; indeed it is often argued that intonation and rhythm play a more important role in effective communication. A balance is required. A teacher may well be tempted to neglect intonation and rhythm because they appear to be harder to teach. This is a temptation to be resisted. A satisfactory combination of the giving of information and the correct rhythm should be encouraged and expected right from the very beginning. Details of tonality contrasts, for example, must be left to a later stage – pronunciation items are to be graded like everything else – but learners must get used to producing utterances with satisfactory intonation and rhythm from the beginning. Obviously they don't have to understand intonation structure before they imitate it.

A teacher with a knowledge of *phonetics* is in a better position to understand and assess pronunciation problems, devise remedies for them, and handle them in class than a teacher without such knowledge. Use of the literature in Further reading, page 118, is recommended. A teacher can also easily gain stimulating ideas and practical examples from published Materials for pronunciation practice; see page 113.

Pronunciation is no more nor any less important than any other aspect of language. Speech is much more than pronunciation – but it is impossible without it! Pronunciation is not the be-all and end-all; *effective communication* is what matters, and this is to be the teacher's constant goal.

References

This list includes all the books referred to in the main text of the book. Some of the books are discussed further in Materials for pronunciation practice, page 113.

Abercrombie D, *Problems and Principles in Language Study*, 2nd ed, (London: Longman, 1963).

Arnold G F and Tooley O M, *Say it with Rhythm*, Book 1, (London: Longman, 1970).

Coles M and Lord B, *Access to English: Starting Out*, (London: Oxford University Press, 1974).

Dakin J. *Songs and Rhymes for the Teaching of English,* (London: Longman, 1971).

Dickinson L and Mackin R, *Varieties of Spoken English*, (London: Oxford University Press, 1969).

Dorry G N, *Games for Second Language Learning*, (New York: McGraw-Hill, 1966).

Hill L A, *Stress and Intonation Step by Step*, (London: Oxford University Press, 1965).

Jordan R R and Mackay R, *A Handbook for English Language Assistants*, (London: Collins, 1976).

Lee W R, *Language Teaching Games and Contests,* 2nd ed, (London: Oxford University Press, 1979).

Mackenzie M D M, *Modern English Pronunciation Practice*, (London: Longman, 1967).

Mortimer C, *Stress Time*, (Cambridge: Cambridge University Press, 1976).

Trim J L M, *English Pronunciation Illustrated*, 2nd ed, (Cambridge: Cambridge University Press, 1975).

Trim J and M, *Sounds Right! A game of phonetic bingo for language learning*, (Cambridge: Cambridge University Press, 1978).

Ttofi C, *Freeway: English for short courses*, (London: Macmillan, 1978).

Materials for pronunciation practice

Trim J and M. Soott R and U. Co. (Pronpunciation,
6th edn (Cambridge: Cambridge University Press, 1979)
Gimson A C, review, *English Language Teaching* (London,
1968)

This section consists of a brief review of teaching materials and courses in English pronunciation that are in print and are widely available today. An item with * indicates that a transcription is used which conforms (more or less) with the more modern system used in this book.

1   General
Publications here include materials for practising the full range of elements of pronunciation – consonants, vowels and diphthongs, word accent (or stress) and rhythm, and intonation.

Arnold G F and Tooley O M, *Say it with Rhythm*, Books 1–3, (London: Longman, 1970–72). A series of three graded readers designed to give practice in all elements of pronunciation (not just rhythm) and transcription. Tape versions available for each reader.

Baker A, *Ship or Sheep?*, (Cambridge: Cambridge University Press, 1977). (*) A good, interesting and comprehensive course. The material is divided into lesson units, each unit containing practice material for individual sounds, rhythm and intonation. Short dialogues are used. An effort has been made to make the course entertaining as well as instructional. It would make an effective remedial course. Cassette version available.

Byrne D and Walsh G, *Pronunciation Practice*, new ed, (London: Longman, 1977). A series of units covering sets of similar individual sounds, word accent ('stress'), rhythm and intonation; each unit contains an initial test ('to establish whether students need to work on that particular contrast'), practice in individual words, pairs and sentences, and a final test. In addition, there is an extra section containing a whole series of tests. A well-planned, thorough and comprehensive course. For elementary to advanced levels. Tape and cassette versions and a separate students' workbook available.

Gimson A C, *A Practical Course of English Pronunciation: A perceptual approach*, (London: Edward Arnold, 1975). (*) An extremely valuable and thorough course. It emphasises the importance of perceiving differences of sound as well as producing them. It teaches a number of phonetic details in the course of the practice materials. It can be used with beginners, but the amount of detail may be beyond the capacity of many. It is certainly recommended for intermediate and advanced learners. It is also very useful for overseas teachers of English to keep their own pronunciation up to standard, and is an important work for those who have a specialist interest in English pronunciation. Both tape and cassette versions available.

Lado R and Fries C C, *English pronunciation*, (Ann Arbor: University of Michigan Press, 1958). A very thorough and comprehensive course, designed as an initial preparatory programme. The material is divided into lesson units; each lesson contains practice of individual sounds and of rhythm, intonation or a special problem, eg the 'reduced' form of *could have*. American pronunciation. Elementary to advanced.

Wright J, *Speaking English*, (London: Oxford University Press, 1973). Two books designed as a remedial course. More attention is paid to combination of sounds than to individual sounds, and a short section on assimilation is included (which is quite rare). Word accent ('syllable stress'), weak forms and intonation are also dealt with. Book 2 contains drills and dialogues. Both tape and cassette versions available.

2 Consonants, vowels and diphthongs

Barnard G, *English sounds*, (London: Macmillan, 1966). A short lively course for beginners.

Barnard G and McKay P S, *Practice in spoken English*, (London: Macmillan, 1963). Designed for remedial work. The material is divided into short sections, ideal for short sessions of 5 or 10 minutes. Cassette version available.

Hill L A, *Drills and tests in English sounds*, (London: Longman, 1961). Pairs of similar sounds are contrasted in individual words, sentences and nonsense items. A well-known and long-established book, which is still very useful for recognising and producing sounds. For beginners and remedial courses. Tape version available.

Mackenzie M D M, *Modern English Pronunciation Practice*, (London: Longman, 1967). (*) Each sound is practised in single words, sentences and amusing little texts; each sound is also contrasted with similar ones. The texts are well written. For intermediate learners. Cassette version available.

Mortimer C, *Sound right!*, (London: Longman, 1975). Each sound is presented both singly and in contrast, in over a hundred well-written dialogues. Just right for elementary learners. Both tape and cassette versions available.

Mortimer C, *Link-up, Clusters*, (Cambridge: Cambridge University Press, 1977). Each of the two books contains 50 well-written dialogues designed to improve fluency by joining up words (*Link-up*), and by practising consonant clusters. For intermediate and advanced learners. Cassette versions available.

Trim J L M, *English Pronunciation Illustrated*, 2nd ed, (Cambridge: Cambridge University Press, 1975). (*) Each sound is practised in individual words and sentences, and is contrasted with all similar sounds. Well illustrated and entertaining. On the whole, too difficult for beginners, but excellent for intermediate and advanced learners. Both tape and cassette versions available.

3 Rhythm and intonation

Allen W S, *Living English Speech*, new ed, (London: Longman, 1965). A well-known and long-established course. It provides plenty of practical exercises with simple explanations of word accent ('stress'), rhythm and intonation. For elementary and intermediate levels. Tape version available.

Cook V, *Active Intonation*, (London: Longman, 1968). A set of lessons for practising the five basic tones in single sentences and dialogues. The tones are given mainly attitudinal meanings. Interpretation exercises are included. For intermediate learners. Tape version available.

Halliday M A K, *A course in spoken English: intonation*, (London: Oxford University Press, 1970). A comprehensive description of English intonation, with plenty of drills for practising all the tones and their variations. It also includes a variety of different types of texts for further practice. Mainly for advanced learners. (The description of English intonation in this book follows Halliday quite closely.) Tape version available.

Kingdon R, *English intonation practice*, (London: Longman, 1958). A brief account of English intonation with exercises, followed by dialogues, prose and verse, with intonation marked. For intermediate and advanced learners.

Morris M, *Speaking English*, (London: University of London Press, 1968). A set of lesson plans for introducing word accent ('stress'), rhythm and intonation, with explanations and exercises. Very helpful advice for both teacher and learner. For intermediate and advanced learners.

Mortimer C, *Stress time*, *Contractions*, *Weak forms*, (Cambridge: Cambridge University Press, 1976–77). Each of the three books contains 50 well-written dialogues to practise different elements of colloquial English. They are ideal for improving fluency. For intermediate and advanced learners. Each has a cassette version available.

O'Connor J D and Arnold G F, *Intonation of colloquial English*, 2nd ed, (London: Longman, 1973). A comprehensive description of English intonation, with a vast array of examples, mostly in the form of responses and comments in 'verbal contexts'. There are also 11 dialogues for intonation practice. Widely regarded as the standard text on English intonation. For intermediate and advanced learners. Tape version available.

Further reading

1 Pronunciation teaching

Haycraft B, *The teaching of pronunciation: A classroom guide*, (London: Longman, 1971). A very practical guide to teaching pronunciation, concentrating very heavily on rhythm and intonation.

MacCarthy P A D, *The Teaching of Pronunciation*, (Cambridge: Cambridge University Press, 1979). A good, sound contribution from a phonetician on the phonetic difficulties in pronunciation teaching.

Renard R, *Introduction to the verbo-tonal method of phonetic correction*, (Paris: Didier, 1975). An interesting, but rather technical, account of training in the perception and discrimination of sounds.

Rivers W M and Temperley M S, *A Practical Guide to the teaching of English as a second or foreign language*, (London: Oxford University Press, 1978). A book that lives up to its title! An extremely valuable publication, especially for the teacher in training.

2 Phonetics and English pronunciation

Cant J P N, *The basic sounds of English: a practical course in RP phonemes*, (London: Audio-Visual English Language Courses International, 1974). A useful attempt at depicting the sounds of English in diagrams alone.

Gimson A C, *An introduction to the pronunciation of English*, 3rd ed. (London: Edward Arnold, 1980). The standard reference book, with detailed descriptions of all the elements of pronunciation.

Ladefoged P, *A course in phonetics*, (New York: Harcourt Brace Jovanovich, 1975). A thorough and comprehensive course in phonetics, well planned and very practical.

O'Connor J D, *Better English Pronunciation*, 2nd ed, (Cambridge: Cambridge University Press, 1979). Perhaps the most readable account of English pronunciation in print, with practical hints and advice for the overseas teacher. Valuable, too, for students and advanced learners.

O'Connor J D, *Phonetics*, (Harmondsworth: Penguin, 1973). An extremely useful account of phonetics in general, with a very readable chapter on the sounds of English.

Prator C H Jr and Robinett B W, *Manual of American English pronunciation*, 3rd ed, (New York: Holt Rinehart and Winston, 1972). An excellent, practical guide to American pronunciation, ideal for overseas teachers and advanced learners.

Wells J C and Colson G, *Practical Phonetics*, (London: Pitman, 1971). A simple, practical introduction to phonetics in general, and English phonetics in particular.

3 Pronouncing dictionaries

Jones D, *Everyman's English pronouncing dictionary*, 14th ed, revised by A C Gimson, (London: Dent, 1977). Generally accepted to be the most authoritative dictionary of Received Pronunciation.

Kenyon J S and Knott T A, *A pronouncing dictionary of American English*, (Springfield, Massachusetts: Merriam, 1953).

Lewis J Windsor, *A Concise Pronouncing Dictionary of British and American English*, (London: Oxford University Press, 1972). A simpler guide than Jones, with usually only one pronunciation given for each word.

Miller G M, (Ed) *BBC pronouncing dictionary of British names*, (London: Oxford University Press, 1971).

Glossary of phonetic terms

The following terms are used in this book without comment or definition.

accent
: 1 An extra degree of energy in the production of a syllable, eg the first syllable of *elephant*. 2 The phonetic aspect of a regional dialect.

affricate
: A sequence of stop and fricative considered as one single unit in the pronunciation system of a langauge, eg /tʃ, dʒ/.

alveolar
: Involving the tip or blade of the tongue and the teeth (or alveolar) ridge, which is immediately behind the upper teeth, eg the articulation of English /t, d, n, l, s, z/.

approximant
: A consonant in which an organ of speech approaches another part of the vocal apparatus, but without causing a closure or friction, eg English /r, w, j/.

aspiration
: A period of voicelessness after the release of a stop, symbolised by a raised ʰ, eg [pʰ].

back
: Involving the back of the tongue in vowel articulation, eg /u, ʊ, ɔ, ɒ, ɑ/.

bilabial
: Involving the two lips in articulation, eg /b, p, m/.

central
: Involving the centre (or alternatively, the overlap of the front and back) of the tongue in vowel articulation, eg /ɜ, ə, ʌ/.

close
: Involving the raising of the tongue to a relatively high position in the mouth in vowel articulation, eg /i, ɪ, u, ʊ/.

dental
: Involving the tip of the tongue against the teeth, eg /θ, ð/.

diphthong	A kind of vowel sound in which the tongue glides from one position to another within a single syllable.
fortis	Used to describe a sound produced with relatively strong muscular effort. An alternative term is 'tense'.
fricative	A consonant in which an organ of speech approaches or touches another part of the vocal apparatus to such an extent that a turbulent air flow is produced, creating friction, eg /f, v, θ, ð, s, z, ʃ, ʒ, h/.
front	Involving the middle section of the tongue in vowel articulation, eg /i, ɪ, e, æ/.
glottal	Involving the vocal cords, eg /h, ʔ/.
labio-dental	Involving the lower lip and upper teeth in articulation, eg /f, v/.
lateral	A consonant in which only the sides of the tongue are lowered, allowing air to pass through the mouth, eg /l/. English /l/ is either *dark*, /ɫ/, when the back of the tongue is raised at the same time, or *clear*, when there is no such feature.
lenis	Used to describe a sound produced with relatively weak muscular effort. An alternative term is 'lax'.
nasal	A consonant in which the soft palate is lowered allowing air to pass through the nose, while there is a closure in the mouth, eg /m, n, ŋ/.
nasalisation	A feature in which the soft palate is lowered allowing air to pass through the nose, as well as through the mouth, eg French *ans*, /ã/.
open	Involving the lowering of the tongue in the mouth in vowel articulation, eg /æ, ɑ, ɒ/.
palatal	Referring specifically to the hard central part of the roof of the mouth.
palato-alveolar	Referring to the forward part of the roof of the mouth, immediately behind the teeth ridge, eg /ʃ, ʒ, tʃ, dʒ/.
plosive	An alternative (British) term for 'stop'.
retroflex	Involving the curling up and back of the tongue tip.
sibilant	A fricative, in which there is a relatively high-pitched hiss, eg /s, z, ʃ, ʒ/.

soft palate	The part of the roof of the mouth further back from the hard palate that acts like a valve allowing or preventing the flow of air into the nose. When it is raised, air cannot pass into the nose; when it is lowered, air does.
stop	A consonant in which an organ of speech completely closes off the flow of air in the mouth, while the soft palate is raised preventing any flow through the nose, eg /p, b, t, d, k, g/.
velar	Involving the soft palate in articulation, eg /k, g, ŋ/.
voice	The vibration of the vocal cords as air passes through the larynx (or 'voice-box'). *Voiced*: accompanied by voice in articulation; *voiceless*: free of any accompaniment of voice; *devoiced*: accompanied by voice for only part of the articulation of a sound.

Index

G refers to the Glossary of phonetic terms, page 119

Index of phonetic symbols